RUGBY CHEEK

BIRMINGHAM MOSELEY BARES ALL

Compiled by
John Duckers

APS Books
Yorkshire

APS Books,
The Stables Field Lane,
Aberford,
West Yorkshire,
LS25 3AE

APS Books is a subsidiary of the APS Publications imprint

www.andrewsparke.com

©2025 Birmingham Moseley Rugby Ltd
All rights reserved.

John Duckers has asserted his right to be identified as the author of this work in accordance with the Copyright Designs and Patents Act 1988

Front cover photograph: Moseley stalwart, the late Alan Adam, reveals more than he might have intended!

Drawings by Kirsteen Snider

First published worldwide by APS Books in 2025

No part of this publication may be reproduced, stored in or introduced into a retrieval system, or transmitted, in any form, or by any means (electronic, mechanical, photocopying, recording or otherwise) without the written permission of the publisher except that brief selections may be quoted or copied without permission, provided that full credit is given.

A catalogue record for this book is available from the British Library

PREFACE

Following the book written to coincide the club's 150th anniversary, it was decided to produce a companion compilation of anecdotes recording the funny, outrageous, strange or even idiotic.

Lots of jolly japes and an eclectic mix of titillating tales from a cohort of young men in the prime of life with high libidos and testosterone oozing from them.

A loose tongue comments: "There could almost be a Moseley book of tales from the nurses' residence on the Bristol Road. And it wasn't a one-way thing – some seemed to collect conquests of members of the Moseley first team squad like Girl Guide badges."

Hopefully an element of truth in all this although, with the passage of time, facts become blurred, names are confused, and dates muddled up.

Maybe a touch of embellishment on my part too!

Mind you, having married a midwife, I do admit to escapades clambering through ground floor windows of nursing homes because the goon on sentry duty was determined to spoil the fun.

No intention to offend – apologies in advance if anything does or anyone has a sense of humour failure. Gentle leg-pulling rather than anything more sinister was always the benchmark.

Thanks to all who have contributed – it was humbling how many from across the whole Moseley/Birmingham Moseley spectrum embraced the enterprise including big names like Nigel Horton and John White from the 1970s and 80s when we were one of the top clubs in the land.

A few myths debunked along the way.

Deliberately, there are no chapters and no date order – down to both promoting spontaneity, inclusivity, and as an incentive to bring all ages together.

For newcomers or those unfamiliar with the club and characters, we have tried to present the stories in a manner that has general appeal to a wide-ranging sports audience, much more than just a bunch of perplexing in-jokes.

Enjoy.

Come on, Mose!

PROLOGUE

I first arrived in Birmingham in January 1990 and promptly took myself along to the Reddings, home of Moseley as it was then.

I knew no one, no one knew me, I spoke to no one, nobody spoke to me.

Felt kind of 'cancelled' in today's terminology, a stranger in something other than paradise.

Nevertheless, it all came good thanks to this particular set of opponents, a Welsh side I seem to recall, though I may be in error.

Now, apart from being rugby fanatics, the Welsh can sing.

When it was time to go, they exited the pavilion on their knees in a long line to the strains of Heigh-ho from Walt Disney's 1937 animated film *Snow White and the Seven Dwarfs*.

Except there were many more than seven.

Heigh-ho, heigh-ho, it's home from work we go
Heigh-ho, heigh-ho, heigh-ho, heigh-ho
Heigh-ho, it's home from work we go
Heigh-ho, heigh-ho
Heigh-ho, heigh-ho, heigh-ho, heigh-ho
It's home from work we go
Heigh-ho, heigh-ho
Heigh-ho, heigh-ho, heigh-ho, heigh-ho, heigh-ho
Heigh-ho

To say it was a spectacular farewell is to underplay it.

There and then, I decided Moseley, now Birmingham Moseley, no longer at the Reddings but Billesley Common, was the club for me.

Gradually I was drawn in and for better or worse, heigh-ho, never regretted it!

John Duckers
Editor

John Duckers

RUGBY CHEEK

BIRMINGHAM MOSELEY BARES ALL

If you've got it flaunt it

Moseley great Nick Jeavons won 14 caps for England 1981-83 and toured with the British and Irish Lions in New Zealand.

Strong, quick, wonderful player in his prime.

But he is also eulogised for a number of unique "firsts" – indeed purportedly a somewhat surreal "threesome".

So, we asked him directly for his comments.

First England player to leave the field in less than one minute.

On his England debut too – against Scotland, at Twickenham. Although a large crowd witnessed six tries in one of the finest games of the season, which England won 23-17, it was not a happy start to Jeavons's international career because he had to come off with an eye injury.

TRUE.

First player to refuse to go out to play in what he viewed as ill-fitting shorts – sufficiently crotchety was he ahead of the 1982 John Player Cup Final, then the pinnacle of English club rugby, that a despairing captain Derek Nutt swopped with him in a bid to sweet-talk his star player into a big performance.

TRUE.

First England player to bring a hairdryer into the Twickenham changing rooms.

Ooh, sweetie!

NOT TRUE.

What?

Didn't dare then put to him allegations that he was so vain he even went to the extremes of putting Vaseline on his calves and thighs. Not to shrug off tacklers but to glint under the floodlights.

Or how on the morning of the 1979 John Player Cup Final he indulged in three shaves to ensure he was looking his best.

Tart!

Jersey japes

It was 1957 and, according to Prime Minister Harold Macmillan us British had "never had it so good".

The Toddlers' Truce, a controversial television closedown between 6pm and 7pm so children could be put to bed, was abolished.

Future members of The Beatles, John Lennon and Paul McCartney, first met as teenagers at a garden fete in Liverpool.

And a Moseley touring side known as the Falcons, consisting of 36 players, including seven first teamers, and a number of supporters, rocked up at Elmdon Airport, now Birmingham Airport, bound for Jersey … they never made it.

Shortly after take-off, the Dakota swerved and crashed, narrowly missing a hangar.

The airport fire crew reached the plane within minutes and put out a blaze in one of the engines. Thankfully, the only injuries were slight cuts and bruises to the pilot and co-pilot.

It must have been terrifying, but, in holiday mood, Moseley made light of it.

Indeed, it was alleged that two players made such a quick recovery they were seen bowling one of the aircraft's wheels down the main runway!

Perhaps apocryphal, but very much in the Moseley ethos.

Other trips to the Channel Islands followed, with the late Taff Hughes confiding how the troops enjoyed "fully experiencing the pleasures that Jersey had to offer".

He added: "The Jersey police must have been charmed by the team as their understanding approach to some of the 'incidents' was probably rather more relaxed than you would find these days."

First teamer Ian Bowland, a 17 year old 'seasoned tourist' on a subsequent jaunt, relates how such 'incidents' just kept coming.

He reveals: "The squad took a particular liking to the 6' 6" concrete policeman stationed in the middle of the local go-karting track.

"Whilst he was concreted down into a huge base this presented a challenge for the group who agreed on the night before we left to rope the poor chap, connect the ropes to our hire cars, and pull him out of the ground!

"This worked a treat and plod was escorted onto the ferry at St Helier in-between two monster second rows (Dave Reeves was one I seem to recall) without the Jersey boat crew taking a second look.

"So far so good and wouldn't he look really rather splendid at The Reddings?"

Time for phase two of the plot.

"The minders assumed their position either side of PC Moseley (he had a name by now) and escorted him through customs and on towards the home bound coach when a very loud 'excuse me' was heard from behind the Border Security desk."

Ooh, er, mother!

Ian notes: "Time for Charlie Smallwood Jnr to earn his place in next year's tour squad and as the son of the head of the Crown Prosecution Service in Birmingham he did a wonderful job of preventing the minders from doing any porridge and ensuring PC Moseley had a return ticket to the Jersey go-kart track."

And they were so close to pulling it off!

A snorting good win

2012 and Moseley travel to Jersey for the island side's first ever Championship game.

A number of supporters fly over to cheer the lads on including Joe Henderson – he and I found ourselves 'sleeping together' (though strictly separately)!

Anyway, Joe takes the view that it would be fun to lift the very large, very posh coat of bruiser Matt Brown.

As they explore the island, the coat starts making personal appearances including on Guy the Gorilla, the much-loved statue to Jersey Zoo's once favourite inmate.

The trip rolls on, Moseley win, the coat is still missing in action and Matt is not a happy bunny.

All one-sided until the troops tell Joe a 'whopper' – that Matt is a cocaine addict and his coat is probably riddled with the stuff. What! And, by now, exhibit A is part of Joe's checked in baggage (had intended to hand it back on arrival at Birmingham Airport) and locked in the system. Irretrievable. Surely, all the evidence a keen Customs officer might need.

Talk of sniffer dogs, visions of being sacked from his job, sweating for hours in the air.

On landing, vision of doom, picks up baggage on carousel, massive trepidation, yet easily clears 'nothing to declare' … complete stitch up.

The cocaine gambit was baloney.

Lots of furious snorting … but not of white powder!

Guy and coat

Joe Henderson (right) and Harley Williams offer a V for victory ... or something like that!

American antics

As part of the USA's bicentenary celebrations in 1977 a rugby union tournament was held in Boston, and Moseley was invited to participate.

But they weren't the only ones.

John Beale, player and administrator, said: "We departed from Heathrow and you can imagine our surprise when it became apparent that there were four other clubs with us on the same plane, including Rosslyn Park, Waterloo and Gosforth!

"With whistles wetted in the departure lounge, by a couple of hours in, one or two of the opposition teams had obviously decided that the flight would be liquid! Anyone who didn't enjoy flying would soon have wished they were elsewhere! A group of about eight players lined up on one side of the plane and ran to the other side, turned, ran back and repeated the effort to try to make the plane rock!

"This was followed by one of the Park players taking over the microphone, acting as the senior flight attendant, and announcing that all drink was free!

"By the time we landed in Boston the passenger deck was completely littered with empty cans, plastic cups and newspapers."

Next came the challenge of getting through customs ahead of the queue.

One of the party allegedly managed it pretending to be an invalid in a wheelchair.

The diminutive Jan Webster, an England scrum half, tried his luck in the kit basket the team had brought with them but stuck his head up at just the wrong moment.

Meanwhile, soon-to-be-capped Maurice Colclough, a huge young man, was to be seen walking up and down, with a massive bottle of whisky, insisting that everyone had a large tot with him!

Interesting character was Colclough.

Having started with Liverpool RFC, he went on to become one of the first Englishmen to play in France, ended up captaining Angoulême, and also later turned out for Wasps and Swansea. He was a member of the England team that won the Grand Slam in 1980 and was selected for the 1980 British and Irish Lions tour to South Africa and the 1983 one to New Zealand, twice appearing in all four internationals.

We digress.

Later, after the authorities had made the bad mistake of allowing the assorted riff-raff into the country, some sort of contrived farting contest shocks one of the locals.

"Are you guys real?" asks the American.

Good question.

It was no surprise when on the return flight Moseley were the only rugby team on the plane!

Say Cheese

Millennials Mark Evans, Alex Hadley, Dan Protherough, Richard Stott et al are paying a visit to the Clothes Show at the NEC.

Plenty of punters trying to sell you stuff along with model agencies seeking the next hunk.

Evo is approached and declines.

But the Moseley wind-up merchants have cottoned on and eventually a lot of hard sell from a persistent 'agency' convinces the lad to change his mind.

A 'studio' is hired, a photographer is persuaded to be in on the act, and a 'photo shoot' is arranged.

Evo, who is living in the same property as Stott and Carl Colvin, proves somewhat deceitful about where he is headed, coming up with the sham excuse that he is off to meet a girl.

So, no mercy.

Multiple pics. "Come on, mate, give us a pose."

And Evo ends up 'semi-naked' down to his boxers and smeared in mud aka the Ab Fab-style randy vision of a rugby player.

Still dreaming of a modelling career until half the first team squad invade the 'studio'.

Evo legs it.

Well fitted up.

Daws and doors

A second team match, Gloucester v Moseley, at Kingsholm … always a tough ask.

John Dawson was captain and prior to the kick-off he was giving it full welly, seeking to fire the troops into a frenzy.

He had played there many times, knew the place like the back of his hand, nothing to be fearful about, the cherry and whites were by no means unbeatable.

And so it went on.

Until a knock on the door of the changing room from the referee to indicate it was time.

Dawson's entreaties reached a crescendo.

Come on, in their faces from the off, big effort from everyone.

Threw open the door … and walked straight into the cleaning cupboard!

Meanwhile, Moseley supporter Cliff Phipps, captaining one of the lesser Old Salts sides, in an away fixture.

Salts are short so he heads to the home dressing room to see if they can spare one or two and so make it more of an equal contest.

Locates the captain. And the conversation goes thus …

"We've only 12 – can you help at all?"

"How many players do you want?" comes the somewhat baffled response.

"Well, ideally, 15."

"I think you're in the wrong place, mate – this is hockey."

Doh!

Snookered by the crowd

The 1970s and 80s were an era when black players were beginning to make their mark.

At Moseley, the likes of Rudy Smith, Colin Osborne and Michael Lawrence, father of England international Ollie, broke through, paving the way for future generations elsewhere such as Jerry Guscott and Kyle Sinckler.

Some in rugby were slow to adjust to such changing times.

An example of this came in a Newport versus Moseley game where the raucous Welsh spectators were never short of offering their opinions on events on the field.

Rudy, a powerful winger, chased forward after a soaring box kick. Making a complete hash of the catch, the ball struck him on the head and rebounded into touch.

Laughter amongst the crowd, then cheers as the referee awarded an attacking line-out to their side.

A pause …

Then a wag, whose second sport was clearly snooker, declared, in seismic valleys burr: "Bad luck Moseley. Seven points away – in off the black."

Much mirth.

Today most would probably condemn the comment as racist albeit the perpetrator probably had no racist intent. I doubt even that Rudy, a lovely, generous, jovial man, greatly missed, would necessarily have taken offence. Different age; different attitudes.

And, anyway, he never let it hold him back as he went on to have a successful coaching career including with Dartmouth Rugby Club in the United States and locally with Malvern RFC.

On his passing, one-time opponent Geoff Stalker paid this tribute.

"I first met Rudy Smith at the bottom of a ruck in the late seventies. He had tackled me with some force and he offered his hand to get me back on my feet. That my whole body hurt and I couldn't breathe was of no matter as I responded to his smile and his old-fashioned sportsmanship. He was playing for Moseley; I was playing for Rugby Lions. He was the one player in the Moseley backs who wasn't an international. But he was the best of them. As a coach, he made every team better. He made every player he coached a proper rugby player and a better man."

Rudy Smith

Shifting sands

Welsh-born winger turned groundsman Alan Thomas never did live down his Sands of the Kalahari pitch of 1989/90.

At the start of the season, The Reddings was dry and dusty and resembled a beach following the application of too much weed killer. Barely a blade of grass in sight.

Despite these problems, the surface held up well and the weather was kind, resulting in not a single postponed game. Indeed, some players commented on how flat and true the pitch was despite its appearance. Only "Tommo" could have got away with it.

And how did he botch things?

Well, not good at reading, it seems he may have confused metric and imperial measurements!

Yet it could have been worse ... as it was for his predecessor John.

Down to a half-tonne roller which was difficult to either pull or push.

Club president Edmund Leach, who had general oversight responsibilities for the ground, cracked the problem.

Ordered John to lean at 45 degrees with the handle strapped to his back and lug the brute like on a canal towpath.

The definition of backbreaking. No health and safety then!

Alan Thomas

The signal to leave

It was winter 1978, and Moseley, including Alan Thomas, suffered a narrow and rare defeat away against London Scottish.

Most of the team (the forwards anyway) were keen to leave early so they could have a few beers in Birmingham.

John Beale recalls: "I went up to captain Martin Cooper and asked him when we were going. At the time, he was the England fly half, and surrounded by women.

"'Why do you want to go?' he said, clearly enjoying the attention of his female fans.

"Nearly everyone wants to go,' I said. Coops retorted with words to the effect that the atmosphere was good.

"'I tell you what,' he said. 'We'll go when Tommo falls over.' Although amused by his decision I thought the likelihood of this was slim, so went to the bar and got another pint.

"About 40 minutes later there was an enormous crash and sound of breaking glass from the end of the room. I looked over to see that a demolished coffee table which had been laden with drinks was the source of the noise, and saw Tommo alongside, getting up from the floor.

"'Immediately Coops shouts out across the room 'saddle up lads, we're going!'"

Spillage!

Everyone out.

Oztracised

The opening sentence in a piece written about a trip Down Under went like this: "Australia and I do not get on. And it's not my fault."

A quip, very much in character, recalled by journalist John Hopkins, of rugby and golf writer Mike Blair, who covered Moseley's glory years in the 70s and 80s for the Birmingham Post, following his death at the age of 91

It, and other wheezes, stand repeating in this book.

Hopkins relates: "I once heard him dictating a rugby report from the press box at Twickenham when the few telephones for journalists were adjacent to a small writing room which was next to an even smaller bar in the press rooms in the old east stand. In other words, a lot of us were crammed into very little space and as the drink was free there was, how shall I put this, a jovial, animated atmosphere.

"Mike's voice had to carry because the connection to a copytaker at his paper might not have been very good – and it did. He didn't hold back, laying into the performance of England, I think it was, with unsuppressed vigour. Come to think of it, as a proud Welshman, he would have relished that and he took it with both hands. Peering over his glasses at some scrawled notes on a piece of paper, and occasionally turning to glance at his colleagues, he uttered one magnificent, damning phrase after the other and when he put the phone down a stunned silence followed. Somebody, it might have been Tony Lewis, then writing for the Sunday Telegraph, said drily: 'Why don't you say what you mean, Mike'?"

And, as a postscript, Hopkins added: "Late one night during the Home Internationals we came up with the madcap idea of rowing from Dublin across to Aberystwyth which I believe is where he was born."

Sadly, it seems, in the cold light of day, the prank was wisely kicked into touch!

Mike Blair

Worst excuses for missing training

Steve Brain – door locked, no sign of life, but caught peeking through the curtains in the hope coach Martin Green had been fooled – he hadn't.

Blazing straddles in time

There is one thing about being "fired up" for a match but Moseley had a tendency to take it literally.

Disaster struck shortly before the start of the 1956/57 campaign, when some painters using blow lamps were preparing the Reddings for the new season.

Burnt wood dropped onto dry wood chippings and, fanned by a strong wind, set the stand alight. Despite the best efforts of the workmen, who formed a bucket chain, the stand was destroyed.

The fire brigade, however, was able to prevent the flames from ravaging the clubhouse, although one end of its roof was damaged.

It happened again 41 years later when honorary secretary, Peter Veitch, was interviewing candidates for the post of commercial manager and heard "a series of small explosions sounding like a lot of fire crackers going off".

He immediately called the fire brigade and 50 firefighters spent an hour tackling the blaze, which had apparently been started by a group of youths. The secretary's prompt action and the efforts of the fire brigade saved half of the main stand but the other half, together with the hut where the players' kit was stored, and two minibuses parked at the rear were destroyed and the changing rooms damaged.

Matters had clearly been jinxed because Peter's interviewee when it all kicked off was appropriately Dave Radburn (get it?) who went on to take a similar role at Birmingham & Solihull rugby club.

"It probably ended up the longest interview ever," jokes Peter.

But all's well that ends well.

The following Saturday's vital National Division Two match, against London Irish, went ahead.

What was left of the main stand was cleaned and made safe, the changing rooms at nearby Queensbridge School were readied, kit was borrowed from North Midlands and the game kicked off, as scheduled, at 3pm. Moseley rose to the occasion and defeated the exiles by 42 points to 16.

Conflagrations were to follow Moseley to Billesley Common.

Indeed the arrival of the 150th anniversary season came with the demise of most of the old corporate boxes on the ground, local youths again to blame for the "match-day" carnage.

Love the sound of breaking glass

In rugby, there are always eccentrics who specialise in strange post-match stunts.

Former Moseley forward and captain David Cathcart, who had also represented both Ulster and North Midlands, later to become club president, was one.

His speciality was eating glasses.

This was on display at the Fighting Cocks in Moseley, Cathy's preferred hostelry, which had particularly thin ones.

If they didn't serve him his second pint quickly enough he would eat the empty one.

Yum, yum. Beats pork scratchings.

Then there was David Genders, a centre and later in life chief selector, whose party trick was to crash through hedges.

Reputedly took out a Grand National fence in a fixture at Waterloo.

But nearly found his own personal Waterloo on an away trip where the coach stopped in a layby so the lads could have a leak.

Challenged to have a go at a particularly thick hedge at the back he took a huge run-up and charged the thing, very nearly making it to the other side, but not quite.

Much to his relief on discovering he would have ended up in a reservoir.

Or it might have been a quarry.

One way or another, a grizzly fate.

PS: One year Moseley stole a one-armed bandit from Waterloo and in the return Waterloo lifted the deer's head (or was it a moose) that graced the Moseley clubhouse.

Deer me, so naughty!

The long and the short of it

Ashley Johnson (left) with fellow veteran, now retired, Jacques le Roux

November 2024 and Birmingham Moseley has a front row injury crisis.

Solution: re-sign as a fall-back (definitely not a full-back) the 38-year-old ex-South Africa international, ex-Wasps, Ashley Johnson, the club's scrum and defence coach.

As cover, just in case …

And, at the same time, pull in tight head prop Henry Feeney, aged 18, ex-Colts, ex-Moseley Oak, Birmingham University.

Only the 20 years between the two. Nothing really.

All of which prompted a string of 1970s OAPs 'hanging on the telephone' (*Blondie: 1978*) expecting late night calls from the 1st XV selection team to summon them for a last hurrah. Meanwhile mothers are pushing babies in their prams around Billesley Common hoping to get a contract offer.

The late late show

It seems in almost every rugby team there is some miscreant with poor time keeping.

In the glory years of Moseley, it was teacher cum farmer and uncompromising hooker Dave Protherough.

He was bailed out at Cardiff by the late, great Sam Doble, England international who died tragically young.

Proth was supposedly on his way. Nevertheless Moseley had to take to the pitch with 14 players and were thankful for an early penalty.

It was inside their own half.

Just then, Protherough appeared and began running across to the pavilion to change.

Doble spins the kick out like a poker player. Fiddling with the ball, lining it up, going back to it and making an adjustment, surveying the posts as if he had never seen posts before – all the time the Welsh crowd getting more and more riled.

And his normal routine took ages anyway as Moseley third teamer Allen Jenkins recalls. "He built a little tee in the turf; readied the ball; stood back to appraise the coming kick; then he walked backwards for five or six steps; one step to the left; took a deep breath; and then launched the ball through the uprights. He didn't care if he was in front of the posts or near the touch line. And he rarely missed."

Finally, as Proth makes his delayed appearance, he gives it the heave-ho and it sails straight between the sticks.

Three points and 15 men.

No such reprieve for Proth at an away match against Nottingham.

No sign of him albeit he later claimed to have broken down on route – a likely tale, though given credence by the state of the wreck he drove.

In fact, being Evesham-based, it seems he was with his sheep on Cleeve Hill where he could graze them for free, it being common land.

Fell asleep – presumably counting sheep.

Yet Moseley still managed to win with 14 men – Protherough had got out of jail again albeit very much in debt to his chums.

PS: Outside rugby circles, Dave was arguably best known for an infamous fight involving Brian Jones, founder of the Rolling Stones, and others when they were at Cheltenham Grammar School.

Roger Gore, school-friend of Jones, remembers: "It has been said that the argument between Brian and Protherough was over a girl but I don't subscribe to that."

Seems more likely they simply didn't like each other.

Known to the school authorities as the "Protherough Affair", it was an arranged contest in the gym that was subsequently broken up by teachers before anyone got too badly hurt.

Retribution followed – one expulsion and three suspensions including Jones.

In some sort of ghastly coincidence, both men were to die in tragic circumstances – Jones, struggling with alcohol and drug problems in the wake of making it big, drowned in the swimming pool of his Sussex home aged just 27 in 1969; Protherough knocked down and killed in 1995 when walking home in an October fog.

Stuck in a Beirut time warp

Antonio Soloman was a quick winger who scored many a try for amateur arm Moseley Oak.

He was admired not just for his rugby ability but, despite coming from a rough area of Birmingham, he was polite, respectful and committed.

Just two faults – always late to arrive and always late to depart.

Hence, in his own way, and 30 years down the line, as exasperating as Protherough.

Gracing Billesley Common was this wreck of a changing room shed, covered in graffiti and consequently always known as 'Beirut'.

It was supervised by a Birmingham City Council employee who, as a side-line, kept ferrets, presumably to counter the smell of the rugby players, tramping in after rolling around in dog shit for most of the game (the locals had mutts the size of elephants and exercised them wherever they pleased).

Anyway, Antonio is last into the showers and last out of the showers.

In fact, so dilatory on this occasion, the groundsman, believing the place had cleared, turns off the lights and locks up, not realising the lad is still in there.

Cue, ten minutes later, a panicked phone call to Oak manager Kathy Duckers.

It is Antonio, pleading to be set free before he is eaten alive by the rats which, given the complete blackout, he could hear but not see. Frightening.

Luckily, she manages to track down the apologetic official and he returns to the scene of the crime.

No evidence though that it taught a relieved Antonio a lesson. Of West Indian origin, time was never a singular consideration.

Kill or cure

Moseley first teamers of the 70s quickly cottoned on to being very cautious about accepting any sort of medical help.

Dai Jones was the sponge man – every club had one.

The magic sponge, they called it, and it came in tandem with a bucket of water.

However, the bucket, especially late in a game, could be full of all sorts – blood and snot, you name it. And, if it was a hot day, don't whatever you do risk a sip of what was dripping down your face for fear of catching cholera.

Don't take liniment from Dai either.

He made up his own version. It was so hot that you forgot about whatever pain you had gone along to consult him about, and, in the showers after the game, it hurt even more when it mixed with water.

As to more professional ministering ... think Rosslyn Park v Moseley with England star Andy Ripley playing for the home side and Dave Warren, Moseley benefactor and one-time captain, for the visitors.

Both got bad cuts requiring five stitches.

Posh boy Ripley was reputedly whisked off to a private hospital for an immaculate job you could hardly see. Warren was treated there and then without leaving the ground – of which only one stitch made it across the wound and the rest missed.

You were stitched up, Dave!

However, with the help of distinguished doctor and long-time Moseley supporter, Joe Jordan, efforts were being made to drag the club's medical arm into the modern world.

One innovation being 'plastic skin', sprayed from an aerosol can, presented to Dai, and of which he was immensely proud.

So, Moseley are away to the much vaunted Llanelli and closing in on a famous win when John Finlan, England international, sustains a cut hand. Quickly, Dai is beside him and out comes the 'plastic skin'.

John White discloses what happened next.

"Finlan holds up his hand, Dai fires the 'plastic skin' at the cut, misses ... and it goes all over the eyes of our best player."

Panic.

Dai desperately scraping off the stuff to enable the blinded Finlan to see again.

Thankfully, Moseley held on for victory.

Fawlty: Where's my bedroom gone?

Being four stars, the Imperial Hotel in Torquay was nothing like Fawlty Towers ... apart from the stories.

Moseley used it for Easter tours until the owners eventually got fed up and banned sports teams.

It was so swanky there wasn't a menu. You ordered anything you wanted.

Dave Protherough put it to the test, asking for shark fin soup for starters with jugged hare as the main course.

Perhaps the best leg-pull though was the occasion when every stick of furniture was removed from hard man Nigel Horton's room and placed neatly on the lawn outside.

Sense of humour failure. Horton, another England international, went berserk.

Get this stuff back or you're dead meat ... and, rather than cross the feared Horton, the culprits, headed by Protherough, did as told.

Wimps.

Mind you, Allen Jenkins remembers one of Horton's first ever games for the club, away at Coventry.

Talk about a baptism of fire.

"Many of the junior players like me drove over to the match in a driving rain storm to cheer on our side. Coventry had a very experienced, tough, looking worse for the wear of many seasons, prop named Phil Judd. It didn't take long for Nigel to put his own physical reputation on the line. Challenged Judd to a fight ... directly in front of the stands in the downpour – to the delight of the cheering Moseley supporters."

Yes, sounds like Nigel.

Nigel Horton

Testing times

To more recent years.

The team are playing London Welsh at Old Deer Park, the drug testers are present, and three players chosen at random will have to give samples at the end of the game.

The unfortunates are Andy Binns, Ollie Thomas and Dean Bick.

As most men will be aware, it is not easy peeing on demand with someone watching your every move.

Thomas and Bick manage but an hour on and to save his life Binns cannot produce a drop.

Two hours pass, the team have eaten their food, had a beer or two and are ready to depart.

Except nothing is still departing Binns' bladder even though he is pouring water down his throat akin to Niagara Falls.

Three hours after the game and finally, thank goodness, urine is sighted. Hurrah! All on the coach ... let's get the show on the road.

But now he has drunk too much water and the sample fails.

Everyone off.

For God's sake Andy, sort your wonky willy out.

It is after 10 pm before it happens – the most unpopular man on the return journey.

Many romantic plans for the night having to be 'Binnsed'!

A surprise elevation

They climbed Everest for the first time using oxygen ... but nobody told John White.

Because he found himself badly in need of the stuff one day with Moseley away at Gloucester and down an injured man in the pack.

Whitey drew the short straw to switch into tight head prop.

"Back in the day, the scrummage was a very different thing and substitutes didn't exist, so when a front row forward went off injured a member of the pack had to move up. As you can imagine, not a task that was relished.

"In those days the only offences penalised were foot up, ball not straight, and dropping onto one knee.

"This meant that tight head props were free to do what they thought was their bounden duty. Which was to get the opposite loose head prop to eat grass, and, failing that, present him with his wings."

A process in which, using neck and shoulders, you sent the guy into orbit, hips about six feet off the ground, ably assisted by his own second row who unaware of the predicament carried on shoving so he was squeezed like a pip.

John continues: "On this occasion I was particularly unlucky because the Gloucester tight head prop, a guy called Keith Richardson, was technically very good and very strong. Having introduced me to the Kingsholm turf, he decided I needed some fresh air and proceeded to pop me out of the scrum.

"As if this wasn't bad enough, with the Shed baying for more blood, their scrum half, a lad called Mickey Booth, yells out, 'want some oxygen up there, Whitey'."

I sympathise. Not a pleasant experience, I can assure you. Never felt so helpless and vulnerable in my life when it happened to me!

Wet wet wet

Birmingham Moseley member John Duckers' rubbish rugby career peaked at the dizzy heights of Aberdeenshire RFC, then in the Scottish 5th division.

Think Moseley Oak on a bad day … a very bad day.

A second team fixture against Elgin-based Moray.

It had been raining all week and consequently there was a 'lake' at one end between the try line and dead ball line.

He recalls: "I was last up from a ruck close to our line and a clearing kick took us to around the half way.

"Unusually for me, I engaged my brain and held myself in check aware our man was racing forward to get his colleagues onside. Sure enough, Moray kicked back long, the ball seemingly accelerating as I desperately tried and failed to get into position. Flicking the tips of my fingers, it spun forward, over the try line, and landed in the swamp.

"Furious with myself, now there was the prospect of conceding a five yard scrum.

"There was nobody within 30 yards of me so I had plenty of time to consider matters.

"I would need waders to touch it down. That didn't appeal. I could attempt to boot it dead but might fail to shift it.

"By now, a fast-arriving opponent was within ten yards of me and there was nothing else for it.

"I dived on the ball, felt for a second that I was drowning, meanwhile creating the equivalent of a tsunami. I came up for air dripping wet and, given the heavy-duty jerseys of the day, red and black colours aka Birmingham Moseley, weighing an extra stone.

"Both teams burst into laughter."

Humiliation!

Oarsome!

Row, row, row your boat,
Gently down the stream,
Merrily, merrily, merrily, merrily
Life is but a dream.

Many Moseley players doubled up as oarsmen in the local rowing club, and, indeed, it was a dream for Dave Warren after he got into using the rowing machine sited under the Reddings stand.

Still looking to keep fit despite middle age.

Set himself targets, and then one day went for the big one – 2,000 metres.

Smashes it; world champion.

"I collapsed ... but once recovered I felt really proud. Determined to tell everyone about my world record."

Except when he double-checked, it turned out to be the record for women over 65 and the real record was half the time.

Always knew Warren was a bit of an old woman!

Confirmed when it was revealed his first love was football and, told on entering secondary school at age 11 he would have to play rugby, he burst into tears!

Dave Warren (left) in his prime

Sheer genius

There was taking the piss off the field and there was taking the piss on the field.

Two examples of the latter from two greats of the game.

Welsh genius Phil Bennett getting over for a perfectly good try in the 1977 Sam Doble memorial game – but then dummying his way back infield, beating two or three more defenders and touching down under the posts.

Secondly, an extraordinary sequence when Sam was at his peak. He was fouled as he went over for a try (4 pts), kicked the conversion (2 pts) and then, having been awarded a penalty kick-off from halfway, popped that over too (3 pts).

Now, that would be a quiz buster.

An Irish ticket trick gets the troops out of a hotel hole

In days gone by, conversation between former Moseley forwards Tony Bertram and John Nolan was likely to be along the lines of "John, if the ref isn't gonna sort out that prop, you'll have to do it".

But there were some well-hidden nascent abilities that were slowly being nurtured in the intellectual hot-house that could be found at Moseley.

Now and again, we caught glimpses.

Take for example the trip organised by former market trader Bertie to Dublin to see the Ireland v England international.

On the boat, big kitty, and Nolan makes himself deeply unpopular with fellow travellers by ordering 90 pints of Guinness, which took a while to serve.

Anyway, loads of mates had been persuaded to chuck in their lot by Bertram's silver tongue on the basis that he had tickets – only to reveal three hours before the game this was no longer the case.

Down to retribution from the troops, the likes of Taff Hughes who didn't appreciate that Bertie had booked the team into this shambles of a hotel, the Harcourt.

Not only a shambles, though decent quality today, but temperance! I mean what sort of tour organiser books a rugby party into a temperance hotel, for goodness sake.

In revenge, Bertram's kit is redistributed around the hotel … unknowingly with the tickets in it. And they disappear. Supposedly. Some doubt they ever existed!

To the rescue came Big John, fresh with ideas and get-up and go. Cardboard signs pleading for spares were quickly created, hung around the necks of everyone in the style of tramps and buskers, Please Help: Tickets Stolen, and all were instructed to drink their way around the Dublin bars in the hope of a minor miracle.

Neary's, established 1887, almost as old as some of the party, in particular comes good

Amazingly, every single person got into the ground and no-one paid more than face value!

Bertie and Big John were surely honing their talents on their unsuspecting colleagues at Moseley.

Jump 40 years to a box at a Moseley v Jersey game, and you would have found the Visiting Professor in Early Childhood at Birmingham City and Wolverhampton universities in deep conversation with the Visiting Professor of Innovation at Birmingham University discussing the challenges of playing in the 1970s.

Clearly, Bertram and Nolan, profited from the sort of education that only Moseley Rugby Club could provide.

An associated tale ...

In the nightclub opposite Neary's, boy band Hill, Petrie and Hill – Jonathan Hill, Gavin Petrie and Steve Hill – discover this woman who is about to get wed and insist on serenading her.

Doesn't go down great.

Petrie clarifies: "She was getting married the next day so we sung her a few songs. Gave her my cap as a keepsake. Except it is during the Troubles and there is this guy looking at us as if to say 'once you've finished you'll be in a black bin liner at the back, pal'."

They had to flee.

"Nolan saved us," says Petrie.

Realised they were in danger.

Never ones to give up in the face of the first setback, they try again a few weeks later when they discover that Nolan has two of his cousins (well fit) over from Ireland ... and are surprised to be serenaded back by the girls who turn out to be regulars in all-Ireland singing competitions.

Subsequently, Gavin and Steve spent several years in rock band Birmingham Rats with ex-Boomtown Rats' Garry Roberts, guitar, and Simon Crowe, drums.

The two Hills and Petrie are still performing semi-professionally around the party and events circuit today under the name, The Moseley Brothers.

Better than being at the bottom of the Liffey complete with concrete collar!

Hillbillies

Hill Petrie and Hill had a go at Opportunity Knocks, the go-to showcase of the late 70s and 80s.

Stardom tantalisingly close.

Gavin remembers: "Our audition brief told us to arrive promptly at 6pm with one song prepared and dressed as if we were going to perform on the actual TV show itself.

"At the time, the Hill Boys were running a car valeting company called Second City Car Valet, which had been originally set up by Moseley stalwarts David Bucknall and Terry Arthur. To continue the Moseley connection, I was working in the printing industry for Gerry Acton, as a sales executive, and therefore my dark blue suit, smart shirt, neat tie and polished shoes would pass muster for audition.

"The Hills on the other hand were very 'hands on' as far as the valeting of cars was concerned, and therefore their M&S V-necks and flared check trousers were often splattered with polish and bits of dusting cloth.

"Needless to say, after a hectic day, they arrived at 5.59pm in full work attire."

Petrie continues: "We'd have probably been better saying we were a singing comedy act but at the end of a stressful working day our powers of creativity were in the red.

"After we sang the Everly Brothers' All I Have To Do Is Dream, the reaction from other performers and even TV staff was hugely positive and we fully expected a second audition. Unfortunately, it was a letter saying 'thank you, but we regret to inform you'."

Perhaps for the best.

He adds: "I think in this modern age the likes of Simon Cowell would have shredded us!"

Opportunity Scruffs

Cleaning up

Back to Bertram …

A loose-lipped chum reveals: "Tony organised a couple of trips to see the Scotland v England internationals at Murrayfield in the 1980s.

"Tickets were easier to get in those days so it was more a case of can we get up to Edinburgh for the game and can we afford it. Well he discovered there was an overnight train from Birmingham to Edinburgh on the Friday night and a return on the Saturday night. This would mean no time off work but a hectic journey, watching the game, booze up afterwards on Rose Street in Edinburgh, and then home.

"But how can we afford this? Well Persil was doing an offer of reduced price train tickets by collecting tokens from the soap powder packets. As the date of the game approached, the collection of tokens from the travelling group was looking pathetically small but 'Headmaster Tony' used his initiative. He got the parents and PTA at his school to collect the tokens and pass them on to him! Problem solved.

"On another visit to Murrayfield, it was decided that we would take a team of veterans and play a game against a local side – I think it was Edinburgh Academicals, but I could be wrong. I don't remember the result but I do remember going back to the clubhouse after the international and as closing time approached Taff Hughes and Dave

Allen were slumped asleep at a table with chairs piled over them so that as soon as they woke there was a tremendous crash."

Ah, Bertie the Braveheart!

Feeling rough

Two rugby-related illnesses unknown to the medical profession.

The first centred on Matson, a club in one of the rougher parts of Gloucester.

The Nomads (3rd team) and Wanderers (4th team) used to play their first and seconds home and away each season and the matches were notorious for the unwelcoming atmosphere, fights during the game and general dirty play which would not be accepted these days.

Consequently, some less resilient players were suspected of catching Matsonitis just in time to miss the fixtures.

Much the same with Pontypool United, a separate club to Pontypool but just as fierce with coalminers and steel workers a plenty. The away fixture brought on Pontypool United flu very early in the week.

Dave Allen remembers: "When the United ended up playing them one Saturday afternoon on a cold and breezy Billesley Common the only time we moved their front row was on the instructions of the ref who wished to avoid the scrum half putting the ball in on to a dog turd!"

Yuch! Too much information, Dave.

Mercurial medic takes his medicine

Mark "Pancho" Davies played in the Nomads or Wanderers in the late 1970s.

Described as a lively and noisy Welsh scrum-half, well-known for sharing rooms with fellow taffy John Richards (Birmingham Moseley director and chairman of Moseley Oak RFC).

It seems that Pancho was also in vogue for his "third-leg exercising which was wonderfully entertaining", but we'll leave that to the imagination.

A mole writes: "Some people may also remember the rather debateable 'not guilty' verdict for driving through a red light following vigorous defence from past Moseley president, the late Charles Smallwood Senior, and some dubious Moseley RFC witnesses."

Better not go there either!

Somewhat surprisingly, none of this held the lad back and he went on to become what might be described as a big knob in the NHS as CEO of Imperial College Healthcare Trust.

My source goes on: "Scampering behind the scrum at Moseley was obviously a key experience in his formative years to enable him to negotiate the tricky politics of the NHS.

"As for his sharing with JR, this undoubtedly helped him understand the potential demand for a good health service."

Ripping yarns

Cheeky!

The late Alan Adam – never a snappy dresser – reveals more than he might have liked on a 1980 tour to Canada.

A facetious parody of him went thus: "Let's call this young tyro Adam Allen. Adam loves the game and joins Moseley to further his playing ambitions with the best club in the Midlands. He is a hooker full of confidence in his own ability, never ever having lost a strike on his own head – unless one of his props has cocked things up! But he has arrived at the club at a time when the 1st XV is flush with excellent hookers."

Consequently, he spent most of his playing career in the lower sides, with the occasional first team appearance.

One such followed the 1973 Moseley centenary dinner.

The 150th anniversary book notes caustically: "Moseley were a little lethargic in the win over Wasps."

Alan went on, in collaboration with Dave Warren, and with the aid of Peter Woodroofe, to save Moseley in its greatest hour of need.

It came in 2002 when Moseley was on the point of being shifted to Oxford, thwarted when Alan put together a putsch.

Dave Warren said: "Alan Adam was the brains behind it all."

Truculent, bolshie, determined, driven, argumentative, loved and loathed in equal measure, he was just the person Moseley needed at the time, though perhaps not the person to take the club on its onward journey.

RIP Alan.

And here is another picture of him, having fallen into a drainage ditch during a litter pick of Billesley Common!

PS: An argument was going on pre-match and quickly an argument was taking place post-match, all involving the usual suspects, James Jowett, John Duckers, Ian Ward and other dullards. Alan's long suffering partner Morag reproaches him. "You're all going on about the same thing you were at lunchtime." To which the reply was: "Probably, but how are we expected to remember what we were arguing about at lunch!" Logic somewhere.

Lost and found

The troops hit the road full of optimism – Cambridge v Moseley.

Driver – Dave Warren, passengers, Steve Evans and Lee Evans.

During the game, centre Tim Molenaar gets injured and is taken to Cambridge Hospital A & E.

Mose are victorious and, after celebratory beer, the players' team coach and the Warro mobile set off for Birmingham.

After about half an hour travelling, Dave's phone rings. It's Molenaar, still at Cambridge Hospital and waiting to be picked up.

Man overboard.

Couldn't really ask the coach to go back and collect him, so, after a few expletives Dave turns the car round.

My mole declares: "There was no other option; we couldn't leave him there to fend for himself ... could we?"

It's been done before!

Think Al Recardo and Alan Hill, to name just two.

Anyway, Tim is collected and the return journey starts again. Tim in the front passenger seat, Dave driving and Steve and Lee in the back.

The source, well in sauce, goes on: "It was getting dark by now and with Dave and Tim chatting away to one another, Steve, who was navigating, nodded off and Lee wasn't far behind.

"After some time, I guess at least an hour, Steve wakes up and is horrified to see a sign saying Doncaster 15 miles. We had obviously missed several turn offs while Dave and Tim were chatting away, each oblivious to which way we should be going.

"After several rounds of blaming one another we eventually arrived back in Brum. A very eventful day."

A word of warning ... wind up merchants often remind Steve of that shemozzle. Gets quite animated while vehemently denying it was his fault.

So, the moral of the story is ... when in his company, for Evans sake, don't mention Cambridge or Doncaster!

Burn baby burn

The kid was as keen as mustard.

Alex Markham was watching a Moseley victory and he had an assignation arranged with a girl who worked in a bookshop run by Dave Warren's wife Jackie.

Presumably intending to turn his evening into a romantic novel.

Just one problem – he'd invited her for a curry and he'd never eaten curry before.

All he knew about the dish was that it was hot ... very hot.

Hoping his date was equally 'hot' and a bit of a dish, he didn't want to mess things up.

Which is where he made his big mistake – allowing Warren to take him under his wing.

Feeling sorry for the emaciated Birmingham University student, he persuaded Enid Smallwood and the kitchen staff to fix the lad up with a spot of post-match grub even though he hadn't been playing.

Asked what he would like, Markham, hoping to replicate the predicted curry experience in order to get a handle on what to expect, asked for a mustard sandwich.

Not a great move.

"He was crying so much the tears were coming out horizontal," remembers Dave.

What a bastard!

Now, you might think Markham would never want to see Warren ever again after being burnt so badly, but fast forward goodness knows how many years and they meet at a Birmingham Moseley v Leeds match.

Markham is now Sir Alex Markham, Professor of Medicine at the University of Leeds, a former chief executive of Cancer Research UK, and, as a member of the Government's Cancer Reform Strategy Advisory Board, reputedly "responsible" for the ban on smoking in public places. Meanwhile, Warro was … er, plain Mr Warren even though he surely deserves a knighthood for services to bad jokes.

No matter, the pair went on a bender to end all benders with not a sandwich in sight.

Pass the mustard.

Sparking a row

Moseley had just got to Billesley Common and weren't at a great ebb.

They were playing Bedford, always hard to beat. The omens didn't look good.

It was a Friday night and, unknown to all, someone surveying potential footings had drilled through an electricity cable.

Everything in the early stages was going as per normal with the sides testing each other out when the inevitable happened … the floodlights partly failed.

And, despite efforts to "bodge" them into life, which got play going again in spurts, they kept failing – stop start, stop start, stop start.

Difficult for either side to get any rhythm.

So much so that as soon as the game had gone sixty minutes, the length of time deemed necessary to allow the result to stand, the exasperated referee abandoned the farce, with the scores level.

An irritated Bedford went home without the predicted victory.

Meanwhile, result! Birmingham Moseley had unexpected points in the bag, 'sparking' wild celebrations.

Worst excuses for missing training

Jim Pullinger – unavailable as the police were trying to arrest him and he was telling them to "come and get me" from the bedroom window.

Keeping it in the family

Dave Warren's kids, Alex, Tom and Joe, would invariably be on the sidelines when dad was performing his stuff on the pitch.

And although then strictly amateur, the game offered some monetary perks.

Such as when Alex ambushed Jim the Guinness on the fruit machine.

Jim, who loved the black stuff, and had been pumping the thing with money, went off to the bar to get more change.

Which allowed Alex to slip in, insert his one measly coin, and it paid out the jackpot.

Jim was not best pleased, but took it with good grace.

Thence, in a follow-up fluke, lady luck extended to the whole team at Warro's company Logmoor as they hit the big time in a money-raising raffle.

Moseley stalwart and car dealer Tim Elt supplied a heavily discounted Vauxhall. Two hundred mini-rugby balls were sold at £100 a time.

The balls are chucked off the Reddings pavilion roof for Jan Webster to catch one and declare it the winner of the motor.

He duly landed the Logmoor contender.

Fix!

When Lee was made to look a right Charlie!

Bet you've never heard the tale of Moseley match announcer Lee Evans being skinned by Aston Villa ace, Charlie Aitken.

A total of 660 appearances for the claret and blues, the most of anyone (Aitken not Evans).

Lee, known as Burlington Bertie to the round ball brigade, was a convert from football to rugby and, like most converts, has been notoriously reticent when questioned about his previous existence.

But I can reveal that he played for Water Orton Old Boys, described as "a dependable left full back – a stopper rather than a creator".

To be relied on apart from the time he was supposed to wash the kit from the previous game and never got round to it.

My spy states: "It was so filthy we had to turn the shirts inside out. But the inside was pink in an era where you didn't wear that sort of colour. Embarrassing or what."

Then came the occasion when they were playing tractor boys Massey Ferguson, who in those days were sufficiently well-endowed they could pull in ex-professionals and semi-professionals.

Including Charlie in the vestiges of his football career.

My man whispering secrets goes on: "Our hero goes in for the tackle, Charlie dangles a foot, and Lee goes flying past. Generously, Charlie lifts him back up."

Better luck next time, son!

So, where did this rugby announcing malarkey come from?

My accomplice tells me: "There was no evidence that Lee had any talent as a sports presenter and, having heard him since, he still doesn't."

Ooh matron, that's harsh!

Lee comments: "In my defence, I was approached by our chairman Mr David Warren to take over from Trevor Corless, who had fallen ill with a throat disorder.

"Dave is not the greatest at giving out compliments and in his own sweet way he said to me 'hey Lee, you've got a big mouth, will you do the announcements for a couple of weeks until we find someone'.

"That was back in 2006, and I am still making a fool of myself up in the gantry, hoping and praying that the opposition don't have any Tongans or Fijians with weird and unpronounceable names. So, by my reckoning, I am getting close to completing 20 years doing the job, not bad for a two-game trial. Especially as no-one has told me when the trial period ends.

"Seriously, I enjoy the job and I think and hope that I have created a friendly rapport with our fans."

Absolutely. We love our Lee.

Catchphrase: "Come on let's hear it for the boys – they need your help."

Lee Evans

Raise a glass to Jimmy

Not many footballers can claim to have won FA Cup medals with two different West Midlands clubs, but Jimmy Dugdale, later club steward at the Reddings, held that distinction.

A solid, dependable centre-half, he was in the West Bromwich Albion side who beat Preston 3-2 in the 1954 final and, having made the four-mile journey to Villa Park for £25,000 – more than £1 million in 2025 money – was back at Wembley three years later, inspiring a 2-1 victory over hot favourites Manchester United.

Lee Evans recalls: "He had many tales to tell and was often comparing the old days and today's spoilt players.

"In his time, on home matches, he would get to Villa Park on a corporation bus, get off at the Holte Hotel, knock back a couple of whiskies and stroll down Trinity Road to the changing rooms to get ready for the game. How things have changed!"

Organised a charity game at the Reddings with Moseley 1st team v Aston Villa Old Stars. David Platt (England, Aston Villa and Arsenal) kicked the match off.

You don't get characters like that any more.

Slaying dragons

Games against the Welsh were always full of incident.

Moseley were playing Newport + the Invisible Man.

(A TV series from the late 1950s featuring a character who looked like an Egyptian mummy from the neck up.)

A mid-week fixture and one of the early first team games involving callow youth Dave Warren.

A Welshman is rucked out of a loose scrum and sustains a head injury – Warren is fingered for the assault. The injured party leaves the pitch. Never coming back surely.

Except late in the game the Invisible Man, swathed in bandages, arrives on the touchline, determined to return to the field, and intent on murdering Warro, who by now is shitting blue lights.

Not for the first time Nigel Horton came to the rescue. First lineout and he knocks out the Invisible Man, who is carted off on a stretcher well visible to all in the ground.

(Incidentally, Newport is where the burly Barrie Ayre proved more than nimble on his feet post match when, after hijacking a local lady, the pair came third in a ballroom dancing contest!)

Thence we move on to another one of those stories with legs, Maesteg v Birmingham.

Ian Bowland, who played for both Moseley and Birmingham, remembers: "Our outside half, not the bravest of individuals, made the fatal mistake of running into the opposition pack who were truly delighted our number 10 had joined them and proceeded to batter him with every fist available.

"Backs tend to be light on their feet and pretty sharp cookies, so our man realised the solution to maintaining his looks was to give the ball to the opposition. The opposition pack immediately gave it back and carried on hitting him!"

John White maintains something similar happened at Abertillery with home flanker Gary Cooper (no, not the Hollywood film star) catching fly half John Finlan man and ball, all over him "like a gorilla", Finlan desperately trying to get rid.

But, perhaps the naughtiest tale was Moseley v London Welsh, 1968, Old Deer Park.

The irascible White was captain.

All he knows is that the kid as the last line of defence was one of the world's most promising tennis juniors who had won the British national junior championship two years earlier.

He tells England international Finlan (and excuse the outdated language) in words to the effect: "They've got a woofter of a tennis player at full back, he's only 18, and it's his first game for London

Welsh. Put the ball up in the air, let's see what he's made of and whether he can catch it."

The "woofter" turned into the legendary JPR Williams who went on to win 55 Welsh caps and eight for the British and Irish Lions!

Invisible Man II

Keith Fielding, England international, playing at the outpost of Hartlepool, home of the monkey hangers.

During the Napoleonic Wars of the early 19th century, a shipwrecked monkey was strung up by the people of Hartlepool, believing him to be a French spy!

Ugh.

Moseley leave on the Saturday for a Sunday fixture so you can imagine the leeway.

Depart Reddings 11am.

Arrive at pub. Leave pub 3pm.

Bus trundles down the road and soon everyone is desperate for a piss.

Nigel Horton says 'no'. There are going to be no stops.

The diminutive Fielding stands up to the monster.

Horton allows the vehicle to pull to the side after all.

Make it to Hartlepool for 9pm despite a 5pm roll call for family billets.

Next day, the pitch is rock hard.

Fielding weaves through brilliantly and is tap-tackled at the last, unbalanced he smacks his head on the frozen surface.

Monkey apparently dressed in a miniature military-style uniform.

Fielding all bandaged up insisting he looks nothing like a monkey or a mummy!

Eee … eee … eee … ee.

Triumphs and tantrums

JC White was coach when Moseley played its final game at the Reddings, its spiritual home, the 37-17 defeat of Worcester Warriors.

Who they?

Regularly throwing foul-mouthed tantrums from the touchline, abusing referees his second sport, stalking the pitch side like a bear with a sore head, glaring zombie-like at opponents, White was in his element.

Andrew Hall, who went from Moseley U10s to the 1XV, 1988-2001 & 2009-2010, had seen it all before, but this was different.

He fondly recalls: "For the squad of 1999/2000, right from the rigours of pre-season all were fully aware that we would be the fortunate few to play on the hallowed turf for the last time.

"When the fixtures indicated our opponents for the season's finale would be our local rivals and rising stars Worcester, we required no further motivation to close the chapter on one of rugby's great club grounds, with such an illustrious history, on a high."

There was only ever going to be one winner.

He remembers: "May 6th 2000 was soon upon us, it was a glorious day, the sun shone, and the pitch was in pristine condition thanks to the efforts of our late and beloved groundsman Tommo. The partisan 3,000+ crowd making the temporary hospitality boxes bounce (and at times threaten to topple).

"A squad that boasted many a legend of contemporary Moseley sides – Pete Buxton, the Sigley brothers, Richard Protherough and Matt Long.

"We were still going in as underdogs with Worcester sitting comfortably at third in the table after only losing a handful of their 26 matches. But, after a rousing and emotional speech by Whitey in the dimly lit and dank home changing room, we were ready for battle. White bellowing from the touchline providing top tips to the referee in language that was so typically cerebrally filthy."

For Andrew, a brace of tries and a man of the match performance. For the team, a triumph of over-achievement. For Whitey, "!#+* off."

PS: Like father, like son.

Ciaran Murphy, known as Machine, of proud Emerald Isle stock, is jumping in a Moseley Oak practice lineout, but the ball slips through his fingers.

Duncan White, son of John, a former Moseley first teamer, hauled in by his father, now Oak coach, to add "punch" to the forward effort, is unimpressed. "If it was a bag of tools you would have caught it, you Irish "!#+*," he informed the building worker.

Not quite the motivational speech Murphy wished to embrace!

Awash with money

Money laundering has long been all the rage in criminal circles, but not many people know Moseley invented it.

The club were raising funds for Guide Dogs for the Blind on the back of the very sad death of Mini and Junior Aaron Boyce.

Ultimately to produce some £20,000, as part of the effort, a memorial sevens was in progress.

This generated £7,000 with the help of organisers James Jowett and his wife Corinne.

So, they get this collection of notes, cheques, silver, buttons and whatever home and place it in a cash box.

Yet such a vast sum unnerves Jowett – what if they were broken into whilst asleep?

Hence, for safety, he hides it away … in the washing machine, of all places.

And, as you can probably surmise, completely unaware, Corinne comes down the next morning and puts the laundry on. Round and round goes the drum and neither is alerted by the cash box clunking about inside.

James recalls: "Subsequently, she took the remnants to the bank and we got all the sodden money back bar about £200."

Not the only story from the Mini and Junior section either.

There's this lad, son of a rugby-mad New Zealander, who keeps playing with a bandage around his wrist.

Eventually he is persuaded to explain what it is all about and reveals that it is there to "keep my hand on".

Blank looks all round including from Bob Brown, then a coach and more recently a denizen of Cobweb Corner, one of the pre-match lunch tables ahead of 1st XV games.

So, dramatically, in front of the open-mouthed Brown and others, he takes the limb off and throws it across the table.

Seems the poor kid's real hand had been lost in an accident and he was determined to keep quiet about his artificial one so he could get a game.

Now that's courage.

Coops and a cunning plan

It was the last fixture of the 1985-1986 season for the unbeaten Nomads side (P26 W26) at Broad Street.

No stone could be left unturned, all was on the line, and Coventry sides were tough.

The illustrious selection team of Alan Williams (skipper), Taff Hughes and David Allen realised some ringers were called for … so hit on a Blackadder cunning plan.

Which involved pulling in an England international pairing at scrum half and fly half.

One plotter was to ring Jan Webster while a second would call Martin Cooper, each saying the other had agreed to play.

To the surprise of the conspirators, the ruse worked.

An even bigger surprise to Broad Street.

Albeit Coops was heard to state on arrival that he'd been conned and no way was he going to be doing any tackling.

No change there then, some might argue, but it did elicit some disgraceful grovelling.

"I will do your tackling, Mr Cooper," squeaked a subservient lackey while licking the great man's boots.

Victory achieved.

And, if Coops wasn't set up the first time, he certainly has been now!

Car candy

First team prop Dick Pearce had a reputation as a bit of a lothario back in the day.

Yes, believe me, the front row brigade, with the handicap of being all gnarled and cauliflower eared, often went to 'great lengths' to pull women, whereas the pretty boys in the backs didn't have to get the finger out, as it were.

So, there he is driving up in the car in order to drop off this girl.

One thing leads to another and soon the pair are engaged in what Private Eye describes as "Ugandan discussions". Until they are rudely interrupted by the sight of the vehicle rolling down the road, Pearce, a PE master at the Oratory, in his lust and passion having failed to engage the brake fully.

Pulling up his pants and racing after it, sadly he fails to catch the runaway motor in time to stop it ploughing into a lamppost.

A case of a hump and a bump!

Worse still, it wasn't actually his vehicle. Borrowed from a pal who had the devil of a job on the Monday explaining to the fleet manager at the then huge M&B brewery that this was all an unfortunate accident and nobody was really to blame. What a Dick!

Medical miscreant unmasked

It was 1986 and Moseley were on a tour of Canada at the height of the AIDS epidemic.

Raging through the world, killing thousands of people who may only have had a few weeks or months from diagnosis to death.

Hosted by Toronto Scottish and put together by Alan Adam, a senior figure in both clubs.

Some heavy hitters among the guests – Andy Johnson, Paul "Gizza" Gisburn and Harley Williams to name but three dubious characters.

An impressive welcome at a restaurant at the top of the CN Tower skyscraper.

Speeches, all 35 tourists in their best frocks, and an audience with the Ontario Minister of Health.

However, diverting from rugby, after the warm-up act, he worryingly went on to emphasise the seriousness of the situation and explained that everyone would have to fill in a questionnaire as to their potential exposure to infectious disease, especially AIDS. Anyone who failed the test would have to pull out of the trip and go home.

Cue gobsmacked and despondent tourists whose jaws hit the floor. What? Except they had been done … it was a complete AA prank, and the Health Minister was a fake.

A case of Adam Intrigue – the Devious Shit (AIDS).

PS: Naturally, tours and sex tend to go hand-in-hand.

In Zimbabwe, the medical advice was allegedly to rub a copper coin between your fingers and, if the lady in question had Herpes, she would jump in the air. A frustrated pervert commented: "This curtailed a lot of sex before the game and was a complete load of rubbish."

More luck in Boston where the local paper supposedly announced: "The Lord Mayor's daughter is going to the Bicentenary rugby party tonight and if she doesn't get laid by a British player she won't go to another party ever again."

That's my type of girl!

Making light of the lily-livered

Not many people know this (as, despite repute, the catchphrase Sir Michael Caine insists he never said), but the term livers and lights refers to the internal organs of an animal, especially when used as food in the shape of offal.

So, a Moseley game is under way, with Nigel Horton captain.

It is around 4pm, floodlights are in their infancy in terms of effectiveness, and it is getting truly dark. "Lights, lights, lights," demands Horton.

To which a wag in the crowd responds: "They're next to your liver."

Williams: You're barred

Welsh great JPR Williams nearly got refused entry to the Sam Doble Memorial match.

Down to keen type volunteer car park attendant, Roger Challinor.

Parking was at a premium at the Reddings, Roger has his list of VIPs, and he is under strict instructions not to let anyone else in.

Up pulls this car and is halted by 'our man on the gate'.

The window is wound down.

"Dr Williams," says a voice from inside.

Roger consults his list … no sign of a Dr Williams there.

Informs the man he will have to park on the road.

"But Dr Williams must be there – he's playing," splutters the driver.

Eventually it is established this is no imposter, but JPR, and he is waved in – bloody jobsworth!

And Roger's defence? "Dr Williams meant nothing to me – if he'd said JPR in the first place of course I would have ushered him through." Roger and out.

Moseley Cuties

Girl power, as with the Spice Girls and others, didn't exist back in the day … or maybe it did, just in different form.

Look at this disco ticket from 1981 indicating how the other half had the upper hand. Albeit would surely be frowned on today as blatantly sexist!

> MOSELEY FOOTBALL CLUB
> *Disco 81*
> at Moseley F. C. Reddings Road Moseley
> on Saturday 3rd October 1981 8.30pm-late
> Members 60p   Guests 80p
> (this ticket admits two ladies free)

Yet more evidence though of who has always been in the driving seat – could Ann Finlan, wife of England international John, 13 caps from 1967 to 1973, claim to be the first WAG?

With a coterie of wives and girlfriends, they sat in the Reddings stand watching their men 'perform' despite most being not that interested in rugby.

So why bother?

"Sixty thighs," Ann allegedly responded.

Indeed, supposedly, there they were giving ratings to players on the basis of their anatomy. The saucy sisters!

Such that the team got a bit sensitive. Seems most of the guys in red and black more or less held their own without going more red than black until another, this time future, international, Nick Jeavons, arrived on the scene.

At 19 and well endowed (I'm still talking thighs here), he blew the girls away. No contest!

Mrs (Colin) McFadyean, Mrs (Malcolm) Swain, Mrs (Kevin) Doyle, Mrs (Gerry) Acton and Mrs (Roger) Holbeche enjoying a good gossip!

An Olive with my gin, please bartender

Birmingham Moseley director Robin Johnson had this mate Ted Olive, both being of Kenyan extraction.

Ted is a doctor at the QE Hospital where there is a virtually free bar for the medical profession.

Takes the lad in for a few beers and talk turns to how best to maximise this opportunity.

No problem, says Olive. Get yourself a white coat and no-one will question your entitlement to imbibe.

Works like a dream for weeks, maybe months.

Until a busybody does pose the question – don't know you, what department do you work in?

Oh, I'm Dr Johnson from maternity.

Bad luck, his inquisitor happens to work in maternity and he knows no Dr Johnson.

End of free drinks. End of 'medical career'.

Going starkers

Streaking and nudity was all the rage in the 1970s.

There were bar games where you casually discarded your clothes in a kind of striptease. Blokes with big bellies ran through the streets with nothing on – not a pretty sight.

Many such antics best glossed over including the Moseley president who ended up stark bollock-naked and dripping in wine at a bar in the south of France.

Perhaps the greatest exponent of this phenomenon was Erica Roe who famously let it all hang out at Twickenham.

Her enormous breasts proved a big hit with the crowd and a double distraction to the England team, it being half-time in the days when the two sides remained on the pitch.

Keeping abreast of the game

Moseley's Nick Jeavons, who incidentally wore his shorts so tight it didn't leave much to the imagination, was one of those ogling her tits. Later modestly claiming that it was the highlight of his career. "Bill Beaumont's team talk went right out of the window!"

Mind you, one for the girls, thanks to Claverdon, whose forte was to throw their naked scrum halves down a lubricated plastic chute to see how many skittles they could knock down.

Sadly, though perhaps for the best, the desire to bare all proved a fleeting distraction as television, the authorities and the public got bored with the exhibitionists.

A bit like Hula Hoops and Pogo Sticks, it was fun while it lasted.

But then there are sometimes mitigating circumstances – like the Moseley rugby tourist who fled his hotel in his birthday suit after an earthquake in the former Yugoslavia.

Now, that's what is called a damned decent, or should that be indecent, excuse.

Former first teamer Roy Kerr explains: "Karl Amatniaks was the naked man fleeing from the hotel (he had been introduced to the Yugoslavian liquor Slivovitz the night before and found it difficult to resist so he probably wasn't at his sharpest).

"He followed this episode with a repeat on a table in a bar in the Yugoslavian town of Sinj when he stripped off to the Zulu Warrior chants. The local host rugby team had seen nothing like this and had assumed, along with the watching crowd, that he would keep some of his clothing on and were shocked when he didn't. This was a strict communist country at the time and they obviously hadn't experienced such treats.

"It was a cheap trip as accommodation expenses were met by the local rugby federation – as long as we brought out a full set of 15 rugby jerseys and some boots. Apparently, these were very difficult to get in such an autocratic society."

President pranks fail to excite

2024 and it seems actually nothing much has changed when it comes to rugby nudity.

How did president Jeremy Summers end up half-naked on the bus returning from Darlington Mowden Park?

Apparently, down to a decent win, a surfeit of red wine and a sing-song.

Personally, I blame former captain Will Safe, who some years back introduced or maybe re-introduced an initiation ceremony for newcomers to the 1st XV, for setting the tone.

Still going.

Ordered to the front of the coach, you have to do a rendition of some well-known song, tell a sexual story (apparently well north of Master Chef's Greg Wallace) and, judged a failure in either test, you get 'paddled' by being whacked on your bare arse as you run the gauntlet back.

Sounds a bit public school to me.

No word of Jeremy baring his arse – in a typical RFU compromise his striptease supposedly stopped at the waist. Good thing too!

Getting the bird

Jonathan Duckers, one of several switchers from Moseley Oak to Harborne, but only after playing more than 100 games for the club, was always sniffing when opponents were throwing miss-passes.

After many failures, he finally gets a classic intercept against Handsworth – on the attack in the Harborne half.

Off he sets, little legs like pistons going nineteen to the dozen, as if he was being chased with a pitchfork by his old Moseley Colts coach Bob Cox, shouting expletives at him all the way.

Cheered on by a massive crowd of 19 plus a dog, as he nears the try line in the clear it is increasingly a matter of running through treacle and a covering winger catches him five metres out.

But can't hold him, both on the floor, and our exhausted hero, still holding the ball, gets up in time to flop over unopposed.

Mobbed by his teammates; spectators in hysterics.

The video goes viral – well at least locally – on social media.

Bravo. Fame at last.

No such celebrating though at another home game when being watched by his dad, John.

Birdy, one of the coaches, is hugging the touchline and realises he is obscuring the view of said parent.

Apologising politely, Birdy, who had put on a bit of timber and was showing a degree of condition, is brutally informed that not only is he in the way but he is "shutting out the sun".

Which post-match lands a surprised Duckers junior with Dick of the Day, and, as punishment, singled out and required to down a pint in one. The sins of the father visited on the son!

Throwing in the towel

Legendary journalist and TV interviewer Gary Newbon – famed for his edgy 'conversations' with Manchester United's Sir Alex

Ferguson, never taking a backward step even when the great man was kicking off – has acted as impresario at a number of Birmingham Moseley functions.

And he has many a tale to tell.

Such as the time he was hosting a gathering of 200 or so sports enthusiasts.

"I got them together and thought, because there were so many, I would start diplomatically.

"Can everyone hear me at the back?"

Big mistake.

"This pisshead responds 'I am afraid I can, Newbon. But I am very happy to swop with anyone who can't'."

A keen boxing fan, it was a case of taking it on the chin.

Mind you, Gary had an interesting way of handling such wind-ups.

Faced with a teaser in the old Birmingham Post John Bright gossip column, a gag that amused him but, he felt sure, wouldn't amuse wife Katie, he resorted to desperate measures.

Spent Saturday morning going round every newsagent in the vicinity of their Solihull home, bought the lot, and dumped them in the nearest skip. Reported back to a somewhat sceptical better half, well used to the wiles of her husband, that every copy had already gone.

Quite what the newspaper's circulation department made of this one-off boom in sales goodness knows!

Off with his pants

Back to the 70s and Martin Green, John White, John Beale et al.

Coaches (the motorised sort) were basic in those days – no toilets – return journeys could be long and the beer would be flowing.

The scam was to pull together a massive kitty and hit an unsuspecting off licence.

For the proprietor, the upside was the euphoria of a bumper payday. The downside was, how shall I put this, the troops' liberal interpretation of the term 'carry out' which often eclipsed accepted accounting principles.

Once back on the coach the drill was that, when the need arose, you peed in a pot and threw the contents out of the skylight – yes, I know, uncouth, but what goes in has to come out.

So, there is Greeny heading down the coach with his pot when he stumbles and spills it all over Whitey.

And immediately goes into Ealing Studios mode and blames the innocent (not very often mind) Beale for 'tripping him up'.

Now a furious Whitey is after JB such that the lad's trousers are chucked out of the skylight, with only his wallet spared by the quick thinking of Derek Nutt.

Somewhere on the A38 to Devon prior to the extension of the M5.

A nostalgic Beale blubs: "I loved those pants – they fitted me perfectly."

Still hope that Birmingham 'TV' archaeologist Alice Roberts may yet find them in one of her digs!

PS: If Greeny and Whitey ever get round to doing a podcast (once someone's explained to them what a podcast is) then we've got a brilliant title for it – Green and White talk Red and Black!

Pulling Macca's plonker

Saturday night drinking culture and 15-20 of the first team squad hit the fleshpots.

Beer, girls, girls, beer.

Backrower Tom McIntosh finds himself attracted to this babe. Nothing materialises, they exchange numbers at the end of the night, and go their separate ways.

But a seed has been sown and his Moseley rugby chums are determined that it should flower.

Somehow, they have broken McIntosh's mobile phone code.

Some text candy develops except the lad isn't communicating with the bird but unknowingly with one of the lads stringing him along.

Starts innocently enough, talk of meeting up for a coffee but the 'wooing' runs for the best part of three months and is gradually becoming bluer and bluer.

It gets to the exchanging photos stage with fake women out of magazines put up to entice McIntosh who in turn provides a shot of himself topless in front of a mirror.

Eventually a rendezvous is arranged, Tom is waiting for the girl to put in an appearance … and the first team squad pounce.

Surprise!

"To be fair, he took it really well," says my source.

Corporate capers

Can't let this opportunity go to waste without a reference to the dodgy corporate boxes at the Reddings.

Let me start with Dick Hickton, a member of the consortium who took over Moseley at the outset of professionalism, who on this occasion was hosting.

Dick was a serial entrepreneur and a colourful character.

A co-founder of Barberry Properties, he was chief executive of Worcestershire-based property company Maximus; a classic car fan, who prior to his passing, had planned to drive a vintage Jaguar from London around the world, stopping off at Auckland, Seattle and Boston, and then back to London on a container ship; and also a chicken farmer producing 120,000 birds every 40 days for Morrisons.

This generated an aversion to chicken.

He had ordered a lamb lunch for the box, so you can imagine the explosion when what turned up? Chicken!

Went into a full-scale rant at the unfortunate who had delivered the hot tray along the lines of 'I didn't order this, the last thing I want to eat is chicken, do you have any idea how many chickens I raise every year, take it back'.

Smoke coming out of his ears.

The lad – almost felt sorry for him, except I was hungry – retreated in what you might call 'a flap'.

Then there was the occasion of the post-match place kick by leading surveyor Glyn Pitchford.

Pitchford was wearing Winklepicker-type shoes aka the Teddy Boys of the 1950s and the scooter-riding Mods of the 1960s ... except this was the 1990s (Glyn was never up with fashion).

So we bet him £20 that he couldn't notch a conversion from in front of the posts wearing his highly unsuitable footwear.

Now Pitchford was a Yorkshireman and you know what they're like with money. Once a note is in their wallet it is truly a prisoner.

Out onto the pitch he strode, tugged a ball from the arms of an eight year old, who looked like he was about to burst into tears, dug in his heel, pointed the ball in the general direction, and began his run up.

It rose drunkenly in an agonisingly slow arc and cleared the bar by a whisker.

Back marched Pitchford to claim his £20 only to find everyone in the box convulsed in laughter and unable to function. Nevertheless, he did receive his prize in the end and the poor kid got his ball back.

However, the award for corporate box lunacy has to go to onetime Moseley Players Association chairman John Nolan who nearly 'killed' his guests when the floor gave way.

In fact, nobody got hurt but they did end up lying in a heap.

To the embarrassment of Big John, a structural engineer no less who went on to become chairman of the Institution of Structural Engineers and a professor at Birmingham University.

Didn't see that one coming, did you John?

You just can't get the staff!

PS: In 2012, Big John – car number plate B1G JN – became president of the ISE. He and wife Valerie facing the ordeal of visiting the 27,000 members in 105 countries around the world, all expenses paid. Gosh, life is tough!

Blowing in the wind

Return of the 70s children who this time are on a coach back from London Welsh.

There were perhaps 20 on board, quite a number opting to stay in the capital for high jinks and other nefarious purposes.

The party are roughly divided into those at the front wanting to keep themselves to themselves, a contingent in the middle who are play fighting, and a card school at the back.

All cool until the play fight ends up with Bill Cranston and Dave Allen – he what pretends to be a serious business type – getting into a ruck that unfortunately takes out the emergency window.

Bits of window bouncing down the M1 never to be seen again.

Oops.

"We thought it was on a hinge," whines Allen, offering one of the worst excuses ever.

Meanwhile the incoming wind has blown the card school's pound notes in all directions, the gamblers desperately trying to retrieve them before they take to the sky.

Naturally, nobody tells the driver what has happened albeit Rudy Smith and Ainsley Bennett, the latter a British former Olympic and World Championship sprinter, both of West Indian origin, where it is a touch hotter, are freezing their pants off.

As is everyone else, mind.

The thing limps down the road until the guy requests that the party 'shut the skylights', there being two.

No-one says anything.

Ten minutes later and the driver rather more emphatically orders: "For *!+% sake, will somebody shut the skylights."

And despite the ruse of one being opened quietly, then closed loudly, the driver smelled a rat.

Pulls into a service station …

Surveys the coach …

"Ah," he reflects.

Martin Cooper claims it all kicked off with Allen and Cranston battering each other with rolled up editions of the Birmingham Post.

Well, at least it wasn't some 'common' rag like the Sun.

Cooper states: "A quick thrust by one of them was deflected by the other but had the effect that both over balanced and crashed into one of the very large side windows. Glass everywhere – in the coach and on the M1. There was complete silence, fortunately no injuries and the driver had not heard a thing. But it was late November and a very cold night with the coach getting colder by the minute.

"Players put on whatever they could find to keep themselves warm but to no avail. As the front few seats closest to the heater were empty, they soon became taken. At this point, the driver questioned his sudden popularity.

"He was relieved and happy to hear from one of the team that the reason for the drop in temperature was that the two central roof windows had been open but he had now closed them (of course they had never been open)."

A few miles later and the driver finally suspects not all is well.

"With his hands turning blue and noses turning red he was worried that there could be other reasons for the Arctic blast. So, he finally decided to pull into Watford services whereupon he discovered the problem.

"As I recall he did not blow his top but simply advised that as the coach was due to be used on the Sunday morning the club would have to foot the bill. He then carried on bringing the team safely back to the Reddings to the warmth of their cars."

Subsequently, according to sources, the coach company go ballistic, vehicle out of action, losing business, etc.

Rumour has it, however, that Moseley administrator Chris Bryant writes them a stern letter.

They had obviously not checked the condition of their vehicle and cannot have maintained it properly, Moseley would pay for the damage, and both parties would call it quits.

No wonder Bryant Homes got to buy the Reddings back in 1998. They clearly knew where the bodies were buried!

PS: No sign of Allen at training on the Monday night! Keeping a low profile. I wonder why!

Pie Eyed

Who ate all the pies?

John Hecht guzzled 15 steak and kidney in one sitting.

A prop, he was also a champion weightlifter.

Big on protein was John.

Good player. Turned out for the North Midlands.

Tucking in

Turkey nugget

It's 2024, England v Australia, and Moseley coach Dan Lavander is on a winner.

Among his many duties is liaising with schools and the RFU are looking to reward such initiative.

Gets invited to the game, free hospitality, well in the trough.

Except a certain amount of research was required … the menu comes through, and Lavvy proves less than savvy.

Has to Google the dishes as no idea what half of them are.

This is an ex-teacher, supposedly an educated man, who most lunchtimes is pretending to be posh – rice, pasta, maybe a couple of superior sandwiches.

Actually, one suspects he doesn't know the difference between pâté and meat paste.

For goodness sake, give the lad a John Hecht pie and chips!

Votre passeport, s'il vous plait, Monsieur Corless

England international Barrie Corless was in charge of this trip to the south of France.

When the squad arrived at the rendezvous point he was acting like the schoolteacher he was in real life. Everyone got a grilling.

Have you got your boots ... have you got this ... have you got that?

Nobody onto the coach without me seeing your passport.

So, on reaching Heathrow, mon dieu, who is the only one to have forgotten theirs ... Barrie.

Or as Derek Trotter might have put it – 'pot pourri'!

Luckily, all was not lost. The authorities rigged him up with a temporary one at short notice and he made it onto the plane.

Tête de veau (everyone's a winner in Trotter French).

Ski Sunday

Links between Camp Hill and Moseley are strong ... evidenced by a particularly special evening long ago yet fondly remembered.

The final of the North Midlands Cup, delayed because of lost fixtures during a hard winter, was held on Wednesday 30th April 1980 at The Reddings between Camp Hill and Hereford.

The late, great Ken Birrell notes in Camp Hill's history: "Contributory to the success was hard consistent training under experienced Moseley players John Beale and Kevin Foreman."

Sessions against the impressive Moseley eight proved ideal preparation, on the day the CH pack was able to achieve dominance, providing excellent possession for the talented back line, and victory was secured 19-15.

Celebrations lasted about a week and spilled over into Camp Hill's Easter tour of Sussex, which proved equally lively.

On field wins over Brighton, Hastings and Lewes, the latter fixture refereed by international official, Roger Quittenton. Off field, staying in Hastings, not a noted ski resort, the lure of the slopes nevertheless proving irresistible.

A tourist reveals: "The hotel manager decided on our last night, to close the bar early. It seems that he'd had enough of us and went to bed. An unfortunate mistake as he now had a group of 20 somethings looking to entertain themselves in his hotel.

"Somebody came up with the idea of upturning the TV room coffee tables to start a series of toboggan races down the hotel's impressive staircase.

"Unfortunately the table legs didn't survive the first race but the tops were used in our own version of the Luge. When even they disintegrated, the planks made passable skis, with rugby boot laces used as bindings."

It was only when Camp Hill's hooker, who had had a spell with Moseley, crashed to the bottom that the manager was finally woken from his slumbers.

My source goes on: "While he was trying to identify the timber used to make the wooden skis, our number two asked if snow was expected."

Yeah, right!

Fortunately, one of the group read how the situation was on the brink of going 'downhill'.

Hid most of the debris in the TV room behind the curtains before the manager could discover the full extent of the damage and the squad somehow managed to escape banishment from the premises.

Worst excuses for missing training

Joe Warren – too knackered, having tried to cycle the 30 miles in from Great Alne in deepest Warwickshire having first inexplicably gone backwards to Alcester to go forwards to Birmingham. No wonder they invented sat navs.

Porridge!

The Wanderers, Moseley's 4th team, are playing Long Lartin high security prison near Evesham.

For any complete idiots, this is naturally an away fixture!

The home side is comprised of both prisoners and guards.

On the Wanderers team is Alan Adam, nickname Killer.

So, you know what's going to happen next. AA has the ball and someone offering himself for a pass and looking to make known his presence, screams 'KILLER-R-R-R'.

And four guys on the Long Lartin side put their hands up.

OK, I'm exaggerating a little … but you get the gist.

And it gets worse.

Moseley's Don Clayton – had a garage, everyone bought their second hand cars off him – is the sponge man, assisting both teams.

He's got his bucket, he's got his sponge, and he has also brought a gallon or two of water.

One of the home team gets injured and is revived with a swig of the contents. Word gets around and soon mysteriously they are going down like nine pins.

Transpires the water container is nothing of the sort but filled with gin and tonic!

Fletch and Grouty would have so enjoyed that one.

PS: Ironically, Long Lartin was always one of the cleanest contests of the year because none of the prisoners wanted to lose the special privileges associated with being on the rugby team. Hard but fair, as Mr MacKay often claimed.

Neanderthal Norman

Moseley are in Toronto, circa 1980s, and amongst the squad is the late Norman Weaving.

Norman was once England Under 16s but didn't grow on and ended up as prop for the third team.

But a seriously hard man, nicknamed Scrap Iron.

There is this young brute, rippling muscles, who is doing in one of the props, screwing the scrum so much that Alan "Killer" Adam tells our man, now well crumpled, that he is being replaced. All in the days when there had to be a genuine injury.

Bloke protests, he is fit to continue, and intends staying on. Killer tells him he is going to the sidelines with a medical condition even if he has to injure him himself.

Norman is then brought into the fray.

His opponent, empowered by having forced a Moseley player out of the game, ups his antics.

He is given a final warning and ignores it.

Next thing he knows is he has a black eye.

But even this fails to deter him.

So, then he discovers he has two black eyes and a broken nose.

After the match, the Moseley party are split up, heading to different Toronto hosts.

So, you've guessed it, who gets Norman, but this poor kid with the seriously messed up face.

Lives with his parents who are shocked at the state he is in. "How could someone do this to you, my darling," wails mother.

Doesn't dare tell her what really happened or Norman would have been out on his ear.

PS: Norman, Dave Allen and another Moseley legend, David Bucknall, are playing in a reunion sevens and gently go down to hit a scrum, which for front row forwards was the highlight of this touch rugby. Then a mobile phone goes off answered by Bucknall who holds up play as he retrieves it from his tracksuit back pocket and quietly says 'may I call you back, I am in a meeting'.

Doble mouths off

The day 1st XV full back, England international Sam Doble found himself in the forwards …

A Staffordshire squad including Moseley second row Ron Morris are in France.

The game proves particularly dirty.

Ron is kicked in the face and badly cut, Arnold Copeland is carried off, Dave Buttery is carried off.

Determined to play for Moseley on the Saturday, despite entreaties Ron, renowned for his straight-talking, refuses to turn out in the next tour match, in the process telling both the coach and the chief old fart where they can stick it.

The result is that Doble, who in a previous life had sometimes played in the forwards, finds himself in the second row.

"He went berserk at me," recalls Morris. "Called me every name under the sun."

But Ron wasn't having it.

Patched himself up and ran out for the Moseley first team as selected.

Nothing woke about Ron!

Pre-season training around 1964/65 inclusive of the blond-haired Doble.

Singing the blues

We're back at Billesley Common now, soon after the move there in 2005.

Mac, garage owner, Newcastle Brown devotee and designer clothes fashionista, has bought at auction a lifelike effigy of the Blues Brothers.

He sets it up on the bank behind the goalposts at the Moseley Forest end of the ground. Sitting on a bench in their top hats.

Tony Kenny, ex-president, foghorn mouth, doing his bit to bolster the club when at a low ebb, is chasing up cheap skates who have scammed their way in ahead of volunteers getting going taking money on the gates.

He spots this lot on the far side, and, jaw jutting, chest out, heads off to confront the cowboys.

Not known to be a big R&B enthusiast is Kenny.

So, he is stomping over, all the while hollering at them, no reaction.

My man in the dark glasses comments: "He must have got within a yard before he realises they are models."

A touch of the blues for TK.

Balder's dash

A Moseley All-Time Internationals team were playing a celebratory game against one of the Leicester junior clubs.

Nick Jeavons, Les Cusworth, Jan Webster ... but unfortunately just 13 turned up.

Typical Moseley.

However, Jeavons' brother-in-law Gary Baldwin was along for the ride, purely as a spectator. Albeit he was an international of sorts – had played for Bermuda, less than 70,000 inhabitants, but, hey, that's mega.

Hauled into the fray. Fancy a game, bro?

OK.

Kit was procured, boots were produced, ankle socks would do, and the burly Baldwin was positioned on the wing.

So, everyone is running out, being introduced over the tannoy – Jeavons, Moseley and England, Cusworth, Moseley, Leicester and England ... and there at number 14 is Baldwin, Bournville and Bermuda.

Who!

Hang on, you can boast about that. A moment of glory.

Indeed, the game was conclusively won and our hero scored a try.

Talking of Leicester, John Liley, 230 games for Leicester, joined Moseley in 1997/98 and Baldwin decided to do a spot of sponsorship.

Paid for a perimeter board to advertise Baldwin Marketing Events with the tag line – More Welly Than John Liley.

First kick and he missed!

Handbags at dawn

Wonderful Welsh three-quarter, prolific try scorer, all round good guy, the late lamented Alan Thomas is on the wing for Moseley in a Boxing Day away game at Coventry.

The forwards do brilliantly, the ball spins down the backs, and Tommo is set up.

The locals are baying for blood, hard to the touchline, screaming for defensive cover, shouting abuse, a female supporter ranting at him.

As Tommo streaks clear, he spies her out the corner of his eye, impromptu inserts his hand through the links of her handbag as he passes by, pulls it from her grasp … and touches down, bag in one arm, ball in the other.

Bagged another one.

Myth?

Sounds too good to be true, even if the sort of tease that would have appealed to a man who enjoyed a spot of mischief and banter.

A different version has no handbag, no try, but some housewife beside the white line who trips him up with her umbrella while he's in full stride.

Who knows?

And, true or false, you could live off this sort of tale for life.

Free beer.

He didn't get mine!

"Tell us again about the handbag try, Tommo."

Man of mystery.

Shirt changed

Talking about deserving of free beer …

Here's another entrant – from Birmingham Moseley member John Duckers and his time in Scotland.

John states: "It concerned an old, long retired international who played for Aberdeen Grammar School Former Pupils RFC in the 1930s and 40s.

"Don't remember his name but the story appears to fit the profile of Donny Innes, who won eight caps, split three/five between pre- and post-war seasons.

"Worth inclusion because it illustrates some of the more absurd elements of the amateur era."

Innes, a doctor, brilliant winger, first appeared in the navy blue in February 1939 against Wales in Cardiff. In those days you had to provide your own shorts, socks, boots … the only thing they gave you for free was the shirt.

During World War II, Major Innes was part of 155 and 156 Field Ambulance units, seeing active service with the 52nd Lowland Division during its push into Germany via Holland and Belgium after D-Day.

When rugby resumed, he was capped again in 1947, captaining his country against Australia. He would captain the side throughout the Five Nations tournament of 1948 enjoying the comparatively rare honour of leading Scotland to victory against England in the Calcutta Cup.

Anyway, his first post-war international and, according to legend, he goes into the changing rooms at Murrayfield with his kit and, there, hanging neatly on pegs, are 14 pristine Scotland shirts. His is the odd one out.

So, he approaches this blazered official, and inquires about why a shirt hasn't been laid out for him.

To which the reply was: "Oh, you got yours in '39."

Had to buy one. Can you believe it? Ridiculous.

That's how strict they were on amateurism.

Nevertheless, a classic tale to dine out on!

You'll never walk alone

Down the years, the Tommo Charity Walk – named after Alan Thomas – has raised huge amounts of money.

Tommo would go round twisting arms and was brilliant at extracting dosh in a manner where you never resented being fleeced!

Lee Evans organised it – at one time a serious 22 miles down the Stratford on Avon canal, participants dropped off at Mary Arden's House charged with returning to Moseley.

Now reduced to 14 miles.

But it didn't always go exactly to plan.

There was the time this young girl somehow got detached from her friends and took the wrong canal fork.

Thankfully, she had the foresight to stop off at a pub, borrow a punter's phone and call off the panicked search that had been launched.

Then there was the occasion when a mate of Peter Veitch fell in.

"A couple of us hauled him out," recalls Lee.

Happened right next door to the Bluebell Inn Cider House in Solihull.

So, perhaps over-eager to wet his whistle.

Well done everyone who has ever taken part.

PS: Not so clever was the occasion of a charity game in which an elderly doctor was so keen that he paid to play. Got flattened in a tackle and had to be taken to hospital in an air ambulance. Ouch!

Rick claims a double

One of the greatest days in Moseley's recent history was 2009 and the 23-18 victory in the EDF Energy National Trophy final over the then moneyed Leeds Carnegie.

However, one man had dual affiliations that day.

The late Rick Coleman enjoyed a 35-year career in education, retiring as the Deputy Head of Baverstock School.

A sports enthusiast, he was a tour guide at both Warwickshire County Cricket Club and his beloved Birmingham City FC.

And that day the Blues had a game.

Which meant a dilemma for Rick.

He solved it by going down to Twickenham with wife Annie on one of the many coaches taking supporters to the 12 noon kick-off and, as soon as it was over, before the celebrations had even started, he was off in a taxi to Watford to see City beat them 1-0.

After the final whistle, they jumped into another taxi back to Birmingham and The Prince of Wales pub in Moseley Village for double celebration drinks.

Goodness knows how much it all cost him, but bound to be a pretty penny.

Showed massive loyalty and just how much it meant to him that Birmingham as a city was achieving things, even though rugby was probably his third favourite behind football and cricket.

Super guy; much missed.

Beasting Bangkok

Back to the tour circuit and, this time, the delights of Thailand.

Not, you might think, one of the foremost rugby outposts, but when did that ever stop an adventurous Brummie.

Or, in this case, posh Brummies, from Solihull.

We're going back to 1980 – thanks to the recall of Dick Goodman, ex-Moseley.

So important was this escapade to the fleshpots of the Far East it generated Press coverage

He reveals: "There were two tours, one for 10 days the other for 14. I was on the 14-day trip and on returning home to where I had left my car there was this report on the back page of the Birmingham Post, I believe sent to the late Michael Blair."

In it, Blair, renowned rugby and golf reporter, mounts a gallant cover-up on the bar girls of Bangkok, but, given the lads never got round to rugby until almost the last day, they must have been utilising their time somehow.

He wrote: "An assortment of veteran Solihull sportsmen, on what might vaguely be called a rugby tour, won their opening, probably only, match against a scratch XV. An exotic confrontation, unparalleled in the history of coarse rugby – one that the Rugby Football Union would probably rather not know about.

"The reason the travellers took so long to get a side into the field are probably too involved to itemise but had nothing to do with the study of native art."

Yeah, right!

He goes on: "One of the difficulties undoubtedly arose from the confusion among the members about just what sort of tour they were on. Some thought they were on a squash tour; others they had gone to play golf.

"Nevertheless, they did the Midlands proud."

The game finished Bangkok 9 Solihull 34.

Bravo chaps!

Corless hands catch Q

Virtually everyone who has ever played rugby thinks they know better than the referee … but, of course, we wouldn't have a game without them.

Rewinding many years, Roger Quittenton was 'the man', regarded, dependent on whose corner you were in, the best and worst of his generation.

Liked to be known as Q – as per the James Bond films!

And Dave Thomas, of North Midlands Society Rugby Football Referees, can reveal some of Q's rugby secret service missions.

Let's start with a Moseley front row incident where we can all have a laugh at his misfortune.

Dave recalls: "At a North Midlands County game at the Reddings I was running the touch for Roger and as a scrum was being set Trevor Corless's arm came swinging round to try and bind with his opposite number but unfortunately he caught Roger bang on the jaw. I saw Roger's legs buckle and thought I would have to take over but he carried on."

Tough guys these MI6 bods.

Plenty more too on agent Roger.

Dave goes on: "The referee's changing room at the Reddings was very small and could not accommodate a 'team of three'.

"Having changed with the home team, I was waiting in the lobby outside when the match doctor wanted to introduce himself to Roger about 25 minutes ahead of the start of proceedings. The doc knocked but all that could be heard was Q running on the spot. No response so he knocked again and again, then tried to open the door. Q quickly asked him to come back at five minutes before kick-off as he didn't want his routine interrupted.

"Next however there was this loud bang from the home dressing room and Q shot out wondering what had happened. It was John White giving his usual pre-match warm-up, having pounded on the door almost breaking the panelling."

Typical Whitey!

Finally, to illustrate that the matey relations between players of today and referees is actually nothing new, he tells this tale.

"While running the touch when Moseley played Blackheath in the John Player Cup, the referee injured himself. I took over for the second half. As is customary, I asked the skipper of the receiving side, Moseley, if they were ready to start again and the response was 'OK Dave'. Fortunately, I had refereed Blackheath more than I had Moseley in previous years so they understood the familiarity.

"There must be something about Moseley as I also had to take over from the Scottish referee who injured himself in an England v Wales Colts game played at the Reddings."

Meanwhile, a couple of asides.

He adds: "Showing how old I am, I first remember refereeing Dave Warren, Derek Nutt and John Beale – what a back row they became over the years – at Belmont Abbey, a school in Hereford which is no longer in existence."

And of the Sam Doble Memorial Match – "to see replacements, all British Lions, rushing onto the pitch as soon as possible will be an image for ever in my mind".

Brilliant stuff, Dave.

Three cheers for the men in the middle.

Whitey is rank out of order

While we are on the subject of both referees and John White ... a tale from the lips of Somerset-based Bob Bannister who was 1st XV line judge during the 1970s.

Didn't actually hear it himself but one that became embedded in Moseley folklore.

"Every time the team were playing in London there was a London Society referee with the compulsory plummy voice.

"In this particular game there was penalty after penalty given against Moseley, perhaps nine in the first half alone."

Until JC White can't handle it any longer, informing 'Sir' that he was having a stinker ... or words to that effect.

Referee marches them back ten yards and then inquires: "How do I smell from here, Moseley?"

Couldn't have been worse than John Moore.

Moseley had been playing Coventry away in the days when the home side always presented their opponents with a barrel of beer.

Nigel Horton declares that nobody is leaving until it is drained.

In the interim, former Coventry legend Jim Broderick, 386 games for the club, who had been in the reverse seconds fixture, turned up and declared that the Reddings pitch "stank".

Actually, it was new signing, pig farmer, Moore!

The eau de cologne of porker wafting liberally on the breeze.

Hang on, though, a funny story about Broderick.

A Justice of the Peace, he'd been walking past an alley when he saw three men in an altercation and rushed over to help the one who was struggling with the other two.

Not exactly being a shrinking violet in the brawling stakes, Jim fought the attackers off sufficiently that the other bloke escaped.

The two dusted themselves down, produced their warrant cards and told Jim they'd been trying to make an arrest.

Oh dear!

John White (right) keeps company with Gareth Edwards

When God intervened

Moseley are playing Birmingham & Solihull, known as the Bees, and a pre-match lunch has been organised in a hastily thrown up marquee.

Local derby, a bit of a grudge affair, plenty of lubrication to give zest to proceedings.

Time to find a seat, announces Peter Veitch, calling to order the assembled throng. A bit like herding cats.

In the process, buttonholing John Duckers and asking (well, ordering) him to say Grace.

Couldn't really get out of it. Panic in Duckers' eyes. Seconds to think of something appropriate.

Then somewhere out of the dark recesses of his tiny mind declared: "For what Solihull Bees are about to receive may the Lord make us truly thankful. Amen."

The place erupts into laughter ... except that is for the away contingent, who are looking thoroughly surly.

Sadly, not a happy ending ... Mose went out and lost.

A sheepish Duckers, looking back, notes: "All my fault. I think the Big Man upstairs decided the comment was sacrilegious and was determined to meet out suitable punishment."

Just one of the many sins Duckers has had to confess!

The charmer in bow tie and braces

There have been many people down the years Moseley through and through, but one of the most distinctive and indeed illustrious must have been Bryan Skeeles.

Always dressed immaculately with his club red and black blazer, braces and dicky bow tie (all red and black obviously).

... until the day he fell into a fountain!

Well known and respected in rugby circles, the first question visiting committees would ask was "where's Bryan?" It was the same when playing away, as he regularly represented Moseley for pre-match hospitality.

Bryan was always polite and welcoming, couldn't do enough for the club and was involved in raising funds for various charities. He was, not only liked and respected by blokes, but also a bit of a ladies man, although always kept under control by his lovely wife Sheila.

The players too had great respect for Bryan, highlighted by the aftermath to an end of season game when all dressed up in Bryan attire (dicky bows, braces, glasses et al).

Bryan Skeeles (left) and Alex Foster ... or could it be the other way round!

Lee Evans comments: "It was brilliant and I don't think Bryan knew which way to look – he was overwhelmed, infectious laugh, everyone loved him.

"There was another occasion when we're playing away against Jersey. Bryan was representing the club as usual. On the follow morning after the game (which we won), the players went out around the town accompanied by Bryan amongst others. Some, celebrating from the day before, were messing around a fountain. Not wishing to be left out, Bryan joined them. Sadly, but hilariously, he fell in, was soaked from head to toe, but happily not hurt."

Carted off to hospital as a precaution but thankfully given a clean bill of health.

Unfortunately, he only had one set of clothes with him. So, the team had a sort around and managed to kit him out in tracksuit bottoms, shirt and hoodie, though no jersey!

Lee continues: "He looked a right sight, a far cry from his normal suave appearance on match days. But obviously took it in good spirit."

On his passing, Rotherham Titans Rugby Club chairman Nick Cragg, said: "Bryan was a stalwart of the club and who for many at the Titans was Moseley Rugby Club. Bryan epitomised all that is great about our wonderful game and he will be sorely missed by all who knew him."

A fountain of rugby knowledge and tradition.

Adam rant gets Sharp shrift from ref

2008 and Moseley travelled down to Plymouth to take on the locals in a then Championship game.

The full supporter squad selection of Alan Adam, former Birmingham Post business editor John Duckers, Birmingham Labour councillor Ian Ward and Moseley veterans Alwynne Evans and Bryan Skeeles were in shipshape condition (not for long) to show off to the sailors.

Crammed into Alan's wreck of a motor known as 'the banger'.

However, some among the away contingent were still smarting on the back of a terrific effort the previous Saturday against the fully professional Nottingham when the lads went down by just two points.

Indeed the wags were still muttering that it was all Adam's fault for their being unable to celebrate a famous victory.

Here is the evidence for the prosecution.

The referee Chris Sharp got a fair bit of 'bird' from the stand at the end of the game. Penalty count not good!

Yet it seems he ran a pleasant B&B in the delightful Yorkshire Dales and only blew the whistle to keep himself fit. Sounds a nice enough guy. So what could have irked him?

'Sir' was spotted in the clubhouse a couple of hours before kick-off getting a dressing down by the 'chief car parking attendant', otherwise known as camp commandant Adam, for utilising the 'blue zone' next to the clubhouse, reserved for the disabled, and told to go and move his car.

Unsurprisingly, it didn't go down well.

One shudders to think how bad the score would have been had Sharp been clamped!

Stand and deliver

Who remembers the Billesley Common 'death' stand?

It was a metal struts and wooden boards affair which prior to the building of the new, albeit not so new anymore, edifice was its predecessor.

Draughty, creaky, far from welcoming.

Nevertheless, some idiot – probably Dave Warren – decided there was still life in the contraption.

So, on successive weekends 'volunteers' – more like slave labourers – dismantled the thing and set it up on the car park side of the ground so as to make way for the new construction. Lugged over there such that most of the dozen or so no longer so young supporters involved nearly had several hernias.

Despite throwing away scores of decaying boards and finding replacements, the move was not a success.

It seems the remainder, deemed adequate, hadn't been, how shall we describe it, sufficiently stress-tested and, after at least one 'victim' fell through as a board gave way, the structure was effectively condemned.

Roped off. Forlorn.

You even needed a life insurance policy when balls kicked into touch and alighting in the ruins had to be retrieved.

Rumour has it that Warren eventually sold it to some football club for a song.

Presumably Rottingdean Village FC in Brighton.

PS: Awkward questions about the origins of the old clubhouse at Billesley Common aren't welcome – it supposedly started out as a hospital AIDS ward.

Cocking up a curry

Moseley v Coventry and Midlands journalist John Lamb, Coventry supporter and sometime rugby writer finds himself after the game at the home of Sam Doble – along with a host of others.

Apart from being an England international, Doble fancies himself as a bit of a cook.

So, he decides to treat the troops to a curry … except he doesn't quite get the recipe right. Specifically the quantity of garlic.

To the culinary ignorant, a clove of garlic is not the same thing as a head of garlic. The head is the entire bulb that's covered in papery skin. When you peel back the skin, you find individual segments — wedge-shaped sections called cloves.

Instead of putting eight cloves of garlic into the mix, arguably over the top already, he puts eight heads in – the equivalent of something like 80 cloves.

Not sure I have ever tasted a garlic curry to that degree – personally I prefer chicken – but apparently, amazingly, it was still edible.

Albeit I wouldn't have wanted to be breathed on by any of that lot for about the next month!

Meanwhile Lammie reminds me of the ferocity of Moseley/Coventry games.

Coventry's international prop Keith Fairbrother is firing up the troops, bringing them to a frenzy, they head out onto the pitch, and on the way he kicks the Moseley changing room door so hard he puts his boot through it.

You'd never describe Fairbrother is 'bootiful'.

Testing times for Jo

Billesley Common has a special place in the heart of Midlands television presenter Joanne Malin … albeit not for the better.

Aged 17, back in 1984, long before Birmingham Moseley arrived, dad gave her a first driving lesson there.

In a blue Austin Allegro – deemed by some to be the worst car ever made, an unreliable, uncomfortable and ugly rust-bucket.

So traumatised she abandoned the whole idea for two years.

And then passed her test in London after just ten lessons.

Reflections on Billesley Common? "I've never been back since!"

A tragedy considering the girl was born just down the road in Meadow View, opposite Swanshurst Park.

Quite the local.

Too long on the throne

Rams away – no, not some sort of sex perverts but a rugby team near Reading.

The Moseley 'charabang' is about to set off from Billesley Common.

All checks complete – kit loaded, roll call of players carried out … full contingent.

Tick, tick, tick.

Coach driver inquires as to making a move.

No problem. Wagons roll.

So, off it trundles, reaches the end of the drive, turns right onto Yardley Wood Road … and a phone call comes in from Ollie Allsop.

He'd sneaked off for a crap and been left behind.

Frantically chasing down the road in a blizzard of lavatory paper trying to attract the attention of the departing bus, which subsequently pulls to a halt.

A shit decision that, eh Ollie!

Staying mum

How mother put her foot down.

Mike Gair, who subsequently moved to South Africa, was an excellent 1960s three-quarter who got as far as an England Trial.

Yet he hid a dark secret that he only coughed to some 50 years later.

Like stars Mike Coulman and Keith Fielding, he could have gone to rugby league for big bucks.

A highly lucrative approach from Warrington, a signing on fee of £4,800 – £100,000-plus in today's money – and employment on generous terms by a practice of rugby league supporting quantity surveyors based in the town.

"I was very flattered," he recalls.

Until he went to see his sick mother.

"I hurried to visit mother in hospital; she appeared to be very weak. I explained the offer I had received from Warrington and mother fired up immediately, straightened in her bed, screwed up her face, and spat out with disgust, 'no son of mine plays sport for money'. And so the offer remained silent and undisclosed."

Oh, the might-have-beens of life.

Mother ... what were you thinking!

Mike Gair

The lady has spoken

Nigel Horton was trying to persuade then England captain Bill Beaumont to leave Fylde and join Moseley.

This was on the basis that he rarely played well in internationals against the Welsh.

And, in Nigel's view, the reason for that was because he didn't have the experience of club contests against Welsh sides whereas Moseley had a fixture list where they played maybe a dozen and frequently beat them.

Nigel recalled: "We were chatting – his wife was there too – after a Wales v England game in Cardiff and I was expounding this theory while encouraging him to switch.

"Until she stepped in and said 'why should he do that when he is already the England captain'?"

A good question and Nigel knew he was beaten.

"They say behind every good man, and Bill's a nice guy, there is a strong woman. But I could see who was the boss!"

Which is how Bill Beaumont never played for Moseley.

Worst excuses for missing training

Jamie Mills – dog afraid of fireworks.

Bog off

Season 2005/6 and Moseley are yet again at a low ebb – National Division Two.

Away, and its's 'grim up north'.

A midden called Halifax.

It has been raining all day. It rains a lot there – around 36 inches a year.

We arrive and it is still raining. The surrounds are a swamp. The team bus can only park in a quagmire. The Alan Adam 'banger' dumped in a morass.

The pitch is like a pudding.

It pours down all through the game, which is utterly dreadful because the ball is like a bar of soap.

Somehow, Moseley win it 22-9 – from memory, down to a fine Neil Mason try.

Time to escape the bog. But, not easy.

Everyone on the team bus has to get out and push it clear; everyone in the 'banger' is required to do the same.

Apart that is from AA in the driving seat, dry, no physical exertion, revving furiously, exhorting the passenger team to greater efforts as the rear wheels spin and they are soaked in spray.

Thanks Al. Had a shower this morning actually.

We got promotion that year – the first and hopefully last visit to Halifax.

Sorry tykes, you've got a wonderful county, but that day it just wasn't meant to be.

West Country wasters

Heard the one about the "Battle of Reddings Road"?

The Moseley United side are playing this Gloucester junior outfit on Billesley Common.

Doesn't matter about the score – lost in the beers of time.

After showering, both sides get back to the Reddings where the 1st XV have been playing Bristol. Into the clubhouse for some food and liquid refreshment.

The Bristol coach is parked up, left foolishly unlocked, and is spied by the Gloucester cowboys who decide it would be nice to ransack it and bring a few trophies home.

No love lost between Gloucester and Bristol.

Except a Bristol bod spies the miscreants and alerts his mates. Who pour out en masse.

Cue a massive fight.

Cops called – someone claiming their sheepskin jacket stolen.

All witnessed by passing referee Dave Thomas who goes into super-hero action.

He remembers: "For some daft reason I grabbed my whistle which was close by in my car and 'blasted away' outside by the coach which seemed to disperse most of the people before the police arrived.

"Tales from the Bristol players subsequently were that they had to stop the coach at Strensham Service station (off the M5) to get some ice lollies to take down the swelling suffered by some of their players in the brawl."

What a load of lolly dollies!

The booze brothers

Moseley legends Pete Smith, Andy Petrie and Robin Shears are having a session in the Reddings.

They eventually emerge well worse for wear.

It is wisely decided that Pete should leave his car and the troops would walk back to his nearby Holders Lane home, presumably for extra refreshment.

Except it means crossing a busy road and in the boys' inebriated condition they find it impossible to detect a gap in the traffic. So, an odd move, but return to the Reddings, ponder the matter, and have another beer.

As you do.

After which Pete comes to the natural conclusion – he will drive home!

Naughty, but, come on, give them a break, the breathalyser wasn't such an issue in those days. And it wasn't far.

Petrie's other great claim to fame was, as a Scotsman, to organise the annual Burns Supper, who, with his wife Pat, he did for some four decades.

Inaugural year, goes swimmingly, a select band of around 50

Second year, not so good.

Shears is supposed to be doing the address to the bard ... he arrives well tanked up, with no notes and probably should have been barred! Disaster written all over it. Speaks a barely comprehensible drivel that has everybody in stiches ... apart from the Petries who are absolutely furious.

Insult to the great man. Could have smashed the haggis over Shears' head.

At least he didn't kill anyone ... which Alan Adam, a dubious kind of anglicised Scotsman, got close to doing.

So carried away with his address that he thrust a knife through the top hat of the chef, thankfully missing his brains, albeit how you would know is hard to tell!

Somehow, though, I think Rabbie Burns would have seen the funny side.

Going Scottish

Barnt Green vino leaves sour taste

OK, we're now onto the one and only Greville Edwards.

Greville was what you call a character, a giant of the licensing trade, big drinker in his own right, prolific ladies man, horny as it comes.

Often two birds in attendance, plus a driver.

Ran the Barnt Green Inn and at the same time sacked and reinstated as Moseley commercial director more times than I've had hot dinners.

All sorts of contrasts – generous, tight, hilarious, curmudgeonly, great company, arsehole.

Forever-finding ways of relieving people of their hard-earned dosh.

So, North Midlands have won the county championship.

"Don't know how we did it – we were slaughtered in two of the games but somehow still found a way," declares Dave Warren.

Against the better judgement of Warro and North Midlands supremo Peter Grace – always used to say grace at Greville's Midlands Sporting Lunch every Christmas (another nice little Greville 'earner') – the go-ahead was given for a celebratory match and dinner to mark this historic event.

Naturally, to be held at the Barnt Green Inn.

Now, separately, 'Grev' has managed to buy a boatload of red wine from France. Presumably on the cheap. Supposed to be top quality but, when it arrives, is far from such.

Solution? He persuades one of the big breweries to sponsor the grand occasion, which effectively means underwriting the plonk.

And they fall for it.

Warro recalls: "It was absolutely horrible. Most people took one drink and that was enough. There were bottles of the filth all over the tables barely touched."

Well, if you thought the connoisseurs spat the stuff out as a matter of course in posh circles ... they certainly did that day!

No doubt, Mr Sneaky gathered up those untouched to sell them off a second time!

PS: Later on Grev always had a box at Billesley Common.

Along comes this 'serving wench' – as he might typically have referred to her – carrying jugs of beer for the corporate hospitality elite.

"Nice jugs, love."

Shooting at sports cars

The revolving turntable now takes us back to 1965ish and Moseley are on tour to the West Country.

Set to play Bridgewater, Exeter and Weston-Super-Mare and staying at a hotel in Cullompton, Devon.

A bit of a chequered history has Cullompton.

In 1678 a local innkeeper, John Barnes was hanged after being found guilty of highway robbery. He had waylaid, with the help of accomplices, a coach travelling from Exeter to London and made off with £600 – a fortune back then. Another local man, Tom Austin, was hanged in 1694. Killed his aunt and her five children. Then murdered his wife and his own two children.

Not even Nigel Horton dealt out that amount of punishment!

Anyway, the tour party, including Alan Cull, were on this coach – a type with sliding windows each side.

Alan reveals: "As we travelled through any number of villages and towns, the tour manager or someone equally important would sit up at the front watching for open sports cars, groups of young people or attractive ladies and shout 'on your right' or 'on your left' and immediately water pistols were drawn and fired out of the appropriate window."

Victims didn't always see the funny side.

He continues: "On one occasion I remember the police stopping us and coming on board asking who was in charge and the important person said he had no idea what was happening at the back of the coach as he was directing the driver!"

Gerry Acton recalls that the police equally took a dim view of the troops disposing of a by now emptied keg of beer. It was rolled out of the coach's sliding door aimed at a German car (World War II still being fresh in the memory of much of the populace) to shouts of "bombs away".

He continues: "From about 1964 I started taking large pieces of white card with us on which messages were written – to display from the back window to any cars that had attractive ladies in them. We usually started with 'We are on Rugby Tour … How are you' and after a few more it always ended with 'Show us your Knickers'! Usually a very successful ploy!"

Back to Alan, who states: "We often had Sunday lunch at the Palm Court Hotel, Torquay.

"On one occasion there was a shout of 'look what I have found in my salad'. Immediately Peter McGowan, a Staffordshire market gardener who knew most things about salads, rushed to the table and announced: 'This slug is not up to standard (for eating)'.

"Immediately a waiter arrived, asked him to keep his voice down and not to disturb other guests."

Which no doubt also applied in the Cullompton Hotel.

Gerry explains: "They always put a dance on for us on the Saturday evening.

"One abiding memory was Peter McGowan, at the bar with his foot on a crate of champagne drinking it from a ladies high heeled shoe!"

Now, that's classy.

Winning the Cheltenham Sevens are (left to right) John Finlan, Gerry Acton, captain Don Lane, Bob Lloyd-Jones, Sam Doble, Alan Corner and Colin McFadyean.

A knuckleduster supreme

Talking about McGowan, a prop for both the 1st XV and the United ... displaying your meat and two veg always produced plenty of unsavoury suggestions from the crowd.

The more nonchalant the more ribaldry.

Allen Jenkins recalls: "After one loose ruck Pete realised he had had his shorts ripped off. The rest of the side formed a circle of privacy as the call went out for a replacement pair. Pete left the circle with not much on below the waist to get the new shorts and put them on in front of the assembled throng. Then the match carried on as if there was no hitch."

That was the era of real men, of course.

And McGowan had a way of getting back at anyone who stepped out of line.

Alan Cull adds: "Peter was a champion 'knuckles' player! I remember him challenging opponents after matches and leaving them with badly bruised knuckles."

Wow! Hurt them on the pitch and hurt them off it.

And it applied to women too.

There was this woman in the latest fashion, knee-high suede boots.

As he was passing her with a pint in his hand, he spilled the tiniest drop imaginable. She lost it and threw a glass of wine over him.

McGowan went to the bar, bought two pints of beer, and poured both all over her. Hmmm. A little ungallant maybe.

But perhaps the best McGowan story was the T-shirt from London Irish.

It was under a glass cabinet, not that it stopped the boy, and it stated: "I am the Mad Hatter of 5th Avenue."

McGowan decided he had to have it and on the bus home presented it to prolific Moseley winger Keith Hatter, who was overjoyed.

Let's say the Irish weren't happy!

Whisky (beer, lager, anything really) Galore

A mission to civilise the renegades north of the border proved a tempestuous affair.

Via a stop-off at Gretna Green where the Sassenach invaders first hijacked a wedding and then produced their own 'wedding'.

Meanwhile somebody had shinned up the flagpole and nicked the Scottish flag.

Peter Veitch, a member of the tour party, explains: "In the late 1960s and maybe earlier, there were two Moseley Easter rugby tours. The 'Senior' tour comprising members of the 1st and United (2nd) XVs went to the West Country, while the 'Junior' tours, made up mainly of the lower Moseley teams, namely the Vandals and Vikings, traditionally toured in Belfast, which resulted in a rather ribald version of the song 'When Irish eyes are smiling'!

"That tradition changed with a Junior tour to Scotland, probably in 1968 or 1969.

"The first stop was en-route in Cheshire, where we were wonderfully entertained by Wilmslow Rugby Club after beating them on the pitch.

"This was the location of the start of the tour's 'crazy theme', namely a game of 'dead ants', which was devised by one of the tourists. Whoever was the 'caller' wore this berry head gear for identification and shouted 'dead ants', at which everyone else, wherever they were, immediately lay flat on their back! Whoever was judged by the berry wearer to be the first down then took over the berry and made the next call."

Not exactly sophisticated, but then rugby tours never were!

Peter goes on: "Needless to say, there were occasions and places when and where it was extremely inconvenient, if not dangerous, to be flat on your back and two have remained in my memory ever since!

"The first was at the Wilmslow stop when I suddenly found myself flat on my back in the middle of a rather busy road in the town! I was mightily relieved when the call came for all dead ants to get up! The other occasion was somewhere near the Border, where we had a 'pit stop' for a beer or three! It was early evening and we were being quite rowdy, when a policeman came up to find out what all the noise was about. I happened to be explaining our 'tour game' to him when the call went up and there I was, flat on my back, admiring the well-polished boots of the policeman just inches from my face. I forget who was the most surprised, him or me!"

So, the tour continued, fortunately without any arrests, and the next stop had to be that well known location of 'runaway marriages', Gretna Green.

Peter continues: "Well, rugby tourists can hardly be there without having a wedding of their own! Unfortunately, I cannot recall who played the part of the bridegroom, but I do know that the late Tony Thomas did a brilliant job of performing the ceremony and my old mate – and business partner of some fifty years – Charles (Charlie) Smallwood acted as the bride, something that I am sure he will deny if ever he reads this, but I will make sure that he does!

"It being a Saturday, there were several proper weddings going on nearby and, in no time, those witnessing these marriages broke off from their serious events to see what was going on and what all the laughter was about. So it was that a considerable crowd had gathered to enjoy the antics of the Moseley tourists and their mock wedding; and it was while everyone's attention was concentrated on the unexpected and noisy entertainment that one of our party (and I can't recall who, honestly!) shinned up the flag pole and relieved it of the flag of Scotland! As far as I know, it has never been seen since and probably remains in a long since forgotten chest of drawers. Any suggestions will be appreciated!"

And that's not it – we're only just getting going.

"That Saturday evening and night were spent in a hotel in the centre of Glasgow. In those days, Glasgow city centre on a Saturday night was not a safe place to be! Even the police patrolled the streets in threes! Not surprisingly, we were literally locked inside the hotel for our safety and had to spend the evening in its bar which, inevitably, we drank completely dry! New supplies were duly procured and rapidly went the same way."

Given the hangovers, Peter's memory, is now getting somewhat fuzzy. Particularly, about the actual rugby.

"As I have forgotten the details of some earlier matches, although I know that I played in one, I now move on to the final destination, Ayr on the South-west coast.

"Unfortunately, our hosts Ayr Rugby Club thought that their opponents were to be Moseley's 'Senior tourists', so they brought in numerous 'ringers' from several other clubs in the region. Not surprisingly, they thrashed us! Conveniently, I have forgotten the score but, as I was our touch judge that day, I spent much of the match behind the posts, watching the succession of Ayr conversions! However, we got our own back in their clubhouse bar afterwards and duly thrashed them in all the silly bar 'rugby games', now sadly long forgotten – or are they?"

Bird brains

The 'dead ants' wheeze had a counterpart – 'flying birds' … as child tourist and subsequent first teamer Ian Bowland found out

His first Junior tour – to Weymouth – and he had much to learn.

"I was amongst an eclectic bunch from the landed gentry and professional types through to genuine hard working grafters representing a wide range of trades and vocations – what an education Weymouth would be!

"We arrived at lunchtime and headed for the market when the tour leader for some reason shouted 'flying birds'.

"What the bloody hell does that mean I thought as one of the multi-millionaires shouted at me to 'get off the ground quickly'!

"The horror and fear in the faces of the market stall vendors was clearly apparent as anybody from 13 to 20 stone plus in our party jumped off the ground onto the stalls and waved their arms around like deranged pterosaurs!"

Last one to comply buys the drinks and gets to make the next call! Monster fun.

Game for a laugh

Talk of rugby bar games brings back shameful memories for John Duckers.

He writes: "Ah, yes, 'boat races,' Fizz Buzz, et al.

"Once got completely legless playing Fizz Buzz when at Dundee University and ended up in a St Andrews police custody cell. Not my finest hour.

"Thankfully, one of my lecturers was pals with the St Andrews' procurator fiscal and I never heard anything more."

That's how drunken rugby mishaps were settled in those days.

"Another jaunt across the River Tay saw us return with the 18th hole flag from the Old Course. And I didn't even play golf! The irresponsibility of youth."

Mike Jones, former Moseley Colt, son of Wimbledon tennis champion Ann, contributes "naked Spiderman" to the mix.

What that?

Well, train carriages and coaches typically have two luggage racks inclusive of floppy webbing running their full length on either side.

The trick apparently (not in my repertoire) is to race along, nothing on, and using feet, hands and other extremities to get from one end to the other in the shortest possible time.

One presumes, given the confined space, it favours small men with small tackle.

Mike would certainly fail on the first count and, if he's any sense, will insist he fails on the second too!

Acton speaks louder than words

It was the Middlesex Sevens and Moseley's Gerry Acton spotted an opportunity.

Nicked all Harlequins' shirts.

Excellent coup.

The troops turned out for training in mid-week emblazoned with the posh boys' attire.

Close, but not quite accurate.

Gerry states: "I did steal a Harlequins shirt from a changing room that was empty and where all their shirts were on pegs. Could have had the lot but only took one, which I still have. I was never asked how I got it but did train in it."

Gerry shows off Harlequins shirt

One suspects it all got hyped up in the telling and re-telling, but still an entertaining tale.

Acton had worked in Birmingham from the age of 16 as an apprentice artist.

He states: "I was getting married in 1962 and going to be living in or around Birmingham. I'd met my future wife Ann at Birchfield Harriers where I had been a member for a few years and occasionally training with (Olympic athlete) Peter Radford and getting quite fit. But until then I was going home every weekend to play for Ludlow Rugby Club.

"So I asked for a trial at Moseley. After early training sessions and two games in the United I got my first game against Sale at the Reddings. I was marking a chap called Shackleton who was a Scottish and Lions player. It was a hell of a learning curve! Next game was against Llanelli at Stradey Park. What an experience that was. From playing on a pitch on the racecourse at Ludlow with 20 spectators to 5,000 at Stradey Park.

"John Wright was my captain in that first year and then along came Don Lane and sparks started to fly."

Talk of sparks flying, Acton was there when a young Nigel Horton was tipped off about how to deal with thuggery. "I remember something from one of Nigel Horton's first games for Moseley. It was against one of the Welsh clubs. We were in the bar afterwards having been beaten and an old Welsh international who was Nigel's opponent told him that if he had smacked him one early in the game so and so wouldn't of happened. Next week he started smacking and never stopped!"

Two more tales from Gerry.

"We went to Dublin, I think to play Bective Rangers, in about 1964 and stayed at the old Jury's Hotel in the centre .On the runway on the way home the engine spluttered and we came back to the hotel. Some players didn't fly home next day!"

And ...

"I was working in sales and on my way back from Cheltenham when I gave a young man a lift. I was wearing my Moseley 1st team tie. He noticed and asked me what position I played. I said centre and he said 'you must be Gerry Acton'. He knew a lot about Moseley before he came to the club. It was Sam Doble."

Sam Doble

Whitey reaches a Peake

Another John White-ism.

When he was coaching Moseley Oak.

Tom Peake, a winger, gets a knock.

Fiona, the physio, tells Whitey that Peake is dizzy and doesn't know who he is.

To which the reply was: "Tell him he is Shane Williams (a prolific Welsh international try scorer) and to get on with it!"

Wait for it though … another shaggy dog tale.

It is the old clubhouse in the Reddings where mutts are banned. Except Whitey cares nothing for such regulations.

Brings in this Great Dane.

And the thing disgraces itself all over the floor. Such that Whitey grabs a broom and starts sweeping furiously.

My mole reveals: "No guilt, no sorrow, just horrible!"

And he used to cram three Great Danes plus himself into a Mini … is that even possible?

Drugs mule

A wonderful illegal story from former Moseley open side George Sey.

It's a tour to Canada and the boys are trying to get through airport security.

George, very black, likes a bit of dope but doesn't fancy getting caught, so slips it into the top pocket of the very white, Ian Metcalfe.

Well, that's Sey's story and he's sticking to it.

Metcalfe, leading Birmingham lawyer, oblivious.

Operating on the principle that a black guy will get searched but a white guy won't.

It worked.

"Metters went straight through and had no idea," says George. "Still doesn't, as far as I'm aware – just a bit of ganja anyway."

Ian comments: "Despite George's view to the contrary, I have heard the story a few times before, and have never quite known whether it was apocryphal or not.

"What makes it even 'worse', at the time, not only was I club captain, but I was also not just an 'upright lawyer' – I was actually a senior Crown prosecutor, employed by HM Government to prosecute cases in the Birmingham Magistrates at Victoria Law Courts. Even more career threatening if it had been discovered…"

And, despite everything, George is still a mate.

"Not only was he a fearless and very quick open side, but he was, and I think still is, a brilliant roofer!"

Sey was from Lichfield and got into rugby by playing the British Bulldogs game in primary school.

Bow-wow-wow.

Worst excuses for missing training

Lawrence Gale – no lights on bicycle.

Just another working day

Players today don't always realise what their forefathers went through just to get to games. Far from the leisurely conditioning and focussed warm-ups enjoyed in the modern era.

Former back Alan Cull still has vivid memories of the crazy dash that marked his first appearance in the Moseley first team.

An employee of Midland, now part of HSBC, banks still opened on a Saturday morning in the 1960s.

He states: "I was selected to play against Gloucester at Kingsholm. "I was at the Cotteridge branch in Birmingham and was not allowed to have the morning off! The Moseley coach left about 11.30am and I had to borrow my father's car and hurtled down the M5. I can still remember the car park gates being ready to open for me, obviously Gloucester having been warned that I would be arriving late."

Moseley supporter John Duckers confirms that this sort of disrupted preparation was not uncommon.

"I can remember my father, Old Birkonians and Cheshire, who worked Saturday mornings for the Cunard shipping line when they were still based in Liverpool, telling me that after half a day at the grindstone he then sometimes cycled several miles to the ground.

"Must have been pretty knackered before he even stepped on the pitch, yet that was how it was. Always felt he should have played for England, but lost it all to the Second World War, hitting the invasion beaches of Sicily, Salerno on the Italian mainland, Normandy and on through France and Belgium to the heart of Germany."

Back to Alan. "I joined Moseley in the 1961/62 season from Five Ways Old Eds as scrum half understudy to Bob Lloyd-Jones. I played initially in the United and later in the 1st XV. I left Moseley at the end of the 1966/67 season when I moved to Liverpool, played for Broughton Park in Manchester for a couple of years and then went to Waterloo where I eventually retired from playing and became a referee."

Now living in Sheffield, he finishes: "I very much enjoyed my years at Moseley and was fortunate to be among some great players, some who have now died, and against some great teams."

Gut instinct saves Mose

1978 and a Junior tour to Malta. The big game was to be against aircraft carrier HMS Bulwark, so, effectively, Moseley v the Royal Navy. Andy Arnott takes up the story: "In preparation, a group of us decided to visit 'The Gut' in Valletta, the evening before the big match, as you would.

"'The Gut' was a steep narrow lane running down from the town to the harbour and was notorious as the Red Light area. We had an interesting visit to many of the seedy bars/brothels going down the hill. Nameless alcoholic concoctions were pressed upon us by enthusiastic women of indeterminate age somewhere well past 50 and it quickly became apparent that the lads were becoming significantly the worse for wear."

Andy, along with Campbell Holden, were becoming a little concerned and decided to maintain a modicum of sobriety just in case.

He goes on: "Over half way down the hill we did a head count to find that someone was missing. George Walters, that wonderful upstanding professional gentleman, long time skipper of the Vandals and much later, treasurer of the Moseley Players Association, was nowhere to be found.

"We set about gathering our somewhat reluctant flock so as to retrace our steps, persevering to the displeasure of the aforesaid 'ladies' who could see the flow of cash into their coffers, slowing alarmingly. We found the miscreant in the back room of a nameless den, clearly unable to string two words together, sitting on an upright chair, surrounded by three or four harridans, with a small child upon his knee, who, it appeared, was in the process of being sold to the unwitting George!"

Andy continues: "A quick exit was the order of the day, so we grabbed our man and headed back up the hill. Angry shouts followed us, together with various nameless objects thrown in our direction. Things became a little more serious when the 'ladies' summoned a group of men shouting and waving what looked like weapons who set off in pursuit. As we were carrying George, they gained on us with alarming speed, and for a moment, things began to look a little tasty.

"However, as we approached the top of 'The Gut', we were much relieved to see a dark coloured minibus with the letters MP on the side and a group of naval ratings in white uniforms. This was the Military Police. Our pursuers melted away and we were able to relate our adventure to our new friends.

"It turned out that the unit was from HMS Bulwark, who were delighted to meet us as several of them were in the team for our match the next day! There followed an invitation to more drinks in The Mess on Bulwark, a ride across the harbour in a Navy launch, and a return to base, which by this time consisted of a concert in a large hall in, I think, a casino.

"I do remember that comedian and actor Stan Stennett (a celebrity of yesteryear who appeared in Coronation Street) was singing, 'I Belong to Glasgow'. The problem was that he only knew the chorus, so in a generous spirit of intoxicated relief, I went on stage to help him out! I think he was very grateful! And, if you are wondering, George still has no memory of his adventure, and in true Moseley tradition, we won the match against Bulwark."

Gassed on the Common

While we are on about George Walters …

Old Griffinians were playing Moseley 4th's at Billesley Common back in the seventies and George was hooking for Moseley.

Not very well, it seems.

Trevor Bow, Old Griffs, reflects: "We had a good pack out that day, or rather a good 7/8 of a pack 'cos I was playing out of position at number 8! We had managed to secure five or six against the head and with about 30 seconds to go, and ahead by three points, Moseley were awarded a scrum under our posts.

"The pack leader urged us like mad to try and win this one and we did. However, it was our hooker's birthday the day before so on the night, he went out and celebrated by having a skin full and a half followed by a Vindaloo at the local curry house.

"Unfortunately, with all the pressure of pushing his heart out, he accidently broke wind and the smell was just unbelievable with everyone almost retching and gagging. Our scrum broke up and the Moseley pack went over for the winning try!

Sun nearly sets on island idyll

A near death experience, underwater cycling and a car called Crazy Horse – all part of Tony Bertram's Malta 1981 Tour "nightmares".

Back then, Malta was about exotic as it got for Moseley.

Tony explains: "In the late 70's and early 80's the 'Junior' sides, who in those days included ageing as well as rising stars, started to get more adventurous about the traditional Easter tour.

"Cheaper air travel meant that instead of a coach trip to the North East, Scotland or the South West, tours went to Malta, Yugoslavia, and the like. As might be imagined, a week away from home in those hedonist times with a bunch of mates playing local teams in 'foreign' parts, preferably with sun, was a perfect recipe for fun and frolics.

Malta 'stash'

"But much skill was involved in setting up a suitable fixture list in a suitable venue. Remember, these were the times when you had to lick an envelope and find a stamp to write to clubs abroad."

This particular jaunt, sponsored in part by Taff Hughes' Netherton-based 'Winnit Boots', included games against the national Maltese team but also the redoubtable Navy champions of the day, the Ark Royal, who happened to be berthed in Valetta. The Moseley team encompassed several former first team players including prop John Dawson, and wingers Roy Kerr, Charlie Smallwood and Alan Thomas as well as former Scottish international back row, Alasdair Boyle.

Tony states: "The rugby was taken seriously and we only lost one match to the local nurses. Amongst us lesser folk were club stalwarts Alan 'Killer' Adam, Taff Hughes, Tony 'Legs' Love, Don 'Mintoff' Clayton, Norman 'Scrap Iron' Weaving, Campbell Holden, and Peter Philpott, all now departed for pastures beyond.

"As might be predicted, there were many misfortunes. It began when the tour operator said he was sorry but couldn't provide the original accommodation, as planned, in Valletta. We would have to stay in a complex in Bourguiba a few miles away. But not to worry, he had arranged that the group should get free rental cars, one between three persons. I think he probably had no idea of the instinctive competitive idiocy of rugby players in general, nor of this self-selected group in particular. I found myself driving a car we called Crazy Horse because it trembled at any speed above 20mph. Alan Adam made a bad mistake of pushing to the front to claim the one convertible, only to discover that if he left the roof down outside a bar it tended to be full of all sorts of discarded stuff when he came out.

"And cars weren't the only point of competition. There was underwater bike riding in the swimming pool starting with head above water in the shallow end and thence on one breath to reach the back wall of the deep end in the shortest time. The SAS raid on the Iranian Embassy was fresh in the memory too having happened the previous summer and there were several drunken attempts to enter rooms through balconies.

Malta squad

"The pitches were very dry and gravelly and in the hot sun we all took salt tablets before the game. The hard grounds were like playing in South Africa."

Which is where it all began to go wrong for Tony.

"The Maltese captain, a very gentlemanly chap, told us he'd arranged to have the pitch watered that morning. Unfortunately, we didn't know he had used contaminated water.

"At some point, I picked up a small graze on my knee, doing some brave jackling no doubt, but next morning my head was hissing and at lunch I blacked out, twice, and finally fell into my soup. Luckily, Dr Boyle, a gynaecologist by trade, accompanied me to A&E and, with the local doctor suggesting I was fainting from the waves of pain from a broken knee, steered him with the measured tones of a Dr Finlay towards a diagnosis of sepsis, insisting that if I didn't get penicillin soon and regularly, I would likely die as the frequency of my blackouts increased."

Sympathetic colleagues evinced some strange concerns.

"My good friend Taff pretended to read the last rights, and I was left in the geriatric ward still feeling woozy, while everyone went off to the game."

No grapes or chocs either.

"Sometime around midnight Campbell appeared with a six pack of Guinness which he insisted was good for me."

Then a reminder of how close he had been, and still was, to being a goner as "nurses brought a wheeled curtain around the old guy in the next bed and his body was removed".

Unsurprisingly, Tony was overjoyed to get out the next day.

"I was released into Alasdair's care with instructions to have a thousand units of penicillin injected every few hours.

"We went to the airport next day, me still in a wheelchair, meeting up with the gang to fly home. Air Malta had unfortunately overbooked and four of us would have to stay behind, all expenses covered in the Dragonara Palace and Casino. It was agreed I would remain as an extra day's recovery would help, Alasdair would need to be my personal physician to inject my meds, Taff, ever caring, insisted he should be my wingman, and Campbell volunteered because the booze would be free.

"Alasdair told me that with this much penicillin, free booze, 5-star accommodation and my rippling physique I would probably never be this invincible again and I should enjoy it while it lasted. Charlie had stayed behind having some local business to attend to, which made five of us sitting down for a free dinner. Of course, it all got seriously out of hand, and when bottles of champagne were being sent to girls in the dining room, the management realised that Air Malta's 'all expenses paid' was probably a mistake.

"At the check-out desk the next day the clerk tapped each purchase into his machine and as the curled tab paper finally rolled full length to the floor, we smiled proudly."

Rugby romp

When Love Island contestant Kodie Murphy joined Harborne RFC, that bolthole for Moseley Oak escapees, everyone thought the club were set for sexy performances on and off the pitch.

After all, he had described himself as cheeky, charismatic, enthusiastic, and a bit of a charmer. "My weak point is I do love a blonde."

Don't we all!

Kodie Murphy

To be fair, he was a decent winger, played five times, and was a good guy.

Then the "influencer", with thousands of followers, winged it off to Dubai to make his fortune in the world of property.

Mum Hayley couldn't believe the state he was in after being delivered back home by the troops following his final Harborne game. "I have never seen him so pissed. He fell through the door and I had to undress him and put him to bed."

Oh well, casa amor, sheik rattle and roll.

Same sort of confusion for ex-Moseley Colt, Henry 'Chits' Chitham-Mosley (surely wrong spelling), who on joining the club found himself in a pre-season game against Birmingham Civil Service and, unfamiliar with his new teammates, began warming up with the opposition

All part of the Harborne mystique – play at Westhill and drink in Harborne cricket club – of being one of the more unruly rugby outfits.

Which on occasion lands them in the brown stuff.

Like the time forward Jordan Bosi "tackled" the festive Christmas tree. As you do – seemed a good idea at the time.

Bar manager Eileen promptly brought the shutters down.

Out!

Minder

The three-quarters tend to hog the glory … but the forwards provide the muscle – on and off the pitch.

Hence, a paean entitled In Praise of Size and Stature from former first team 'girl' Roy Kerr.

He explains: "I come from an era when wingers weren't all trying to be Jonah Lomu-reincarnate, scrum-halves scampered around like mice with Ralgex in their jock-strap and a hooker would hang from sturdy props like a swing in a children's playground. However, we were part of a team and, on the pitch, you could rely on the heavyweight forwards to use their size and stature to protect lesser mortals from potential on-field intimidation and violence.

"Off-field their re-assuring presence wasn't always at hand when it was needed but when the cavalry did arrive all would be OK."

Example One.

The now-departed Alan Adam is in Toronto on one of the wonderful Moseley Junior tours.

Roy states: "After a recreational afternoon comprising a few drinks and some sight-seeing several of us vertically-challenged team members were catching the underground back to our lodgings in the company of our brethren from the pack. Alan was feeling brave after his imbibing and especially with back-up all around.

"It was rush-hour and we were packed standing by the door. The train stopped but there was only room for one person to get on and a burly city gent barged the girl who was nearest out of the way.

"Alan watched this and said to the man in a loud voice so that the whole carriage could hear 'You sure put her in her place'."

The man smiled back.

"Just a pity she stole your wallet as you got on."

The whole carriage erupted in laughter whilst the city gent slunk away.

Example Two.

"On away trips to one of the London clubs we always used to stop at the motorway service stations for a break and refreshment. On one occasion, it was evening and we arrived at Watford Gap at the same time as a coachload of football supporters – not sure if they were Blues or Villa but they were definitely from Birmingham.

"I was patiently queuing for my coffee when about three of them jumped in front of me. I politely pointed out that there was a queue and they should join it from the back. At this point, they squared up to me with a blunt 'We are not moving, so what are you going to do about it'?

"Then the big guns arrived in the form of two of my more sizeable team-mates including second row Les Smith.

"Les asked if I was having any problems."

Immediate change of tune from the football supporters, insisting they were just wanting to buy their newly-acquired buddy a cup of coffee.

Roy goes on: "I very much enjoyed their free cup of coffee and the reassurance of having some team-mates of a size and stature that ensured the evening passed without incident."

Me thinks the baby-sitting of three-quarters by their burlier brethren will go on as long as rugby exists!

More than a bullshitter

In 2022 Dan Lewis was Birmingham Moseley's fly half and an excellent player he was too.

But it took red and black to turn entirely red before his career took off big time.

What am I talking about?

Well, his side-line for the club was a ramping up of the social media output and it did not go unnoticed.

At the end of that season, he spent a year at Leicester Lions, and then traded in a lion for a bull!

Specifically joining Oracle Red Bull Racing as social media executive.

What an opportunity for the man who floated via Colchester RFC, Northampton, Bedford, Saracens, French side Oyonnax, Cambridge, North Otago in New Zealand and Coventry.

Quite some travelling, but nothing like going round the world with the motor racing circus.

Red Bull gives you wings.

Well, sort of, a US legal row back in 2014 suggesting this was a load of baloney. Red Bull settled out of court and inserted an extra 'i'.

So Red Bull now gives you wiings … though goodness knows what that means.

Leaving Dan to 'wiing' it!

Raise a glass to Broughy

Ale have another pint please

I know beer is synonymous with rugby … but Birmingham Moseley went the extra mile when in 2023 they signed Dan Brough.

His family run the All Nations pub and brewery in Madeley, close to both Telford and the historic Ironbridge, home to the Industrial Revolution.

All Nations Bitter and Eliza Lewis Light Ale.

Until relatively recently, prior to the explosion of micro-breweries, one of the famous last four brewhouses left in England, established in 1832.

The others being the Three Tuns in Bishops Castle, Ma Pardoe's in Netherton, Dudley, and the Blue Anchor, Helston in Cornwall.

Quite a pub crawl ... and Dan has done his own rugby cum pub crawl via Bridgnorth, Newport, Cambridge, Benfica in Portugal, also representing Hungary in both 7's and 15's .

Clearly 'hungary' for more rugby success.

And the beer?

"Tasty," declares Chris Bertram, CAMRA member, beer aficionado and the guy who puts Moseley Matters together. "I would definitely recommend it." I'll drink to that!

There's always a Nigel

As Christopher Robin might say, a return to the Poo Corner of the Mini and Juniors.

Nigel Stelling, brainy, Moseley man, big style criminal lawyer in Birmingham, is overseeing the team's trip down to the Richmond Festival, circa the late 1990s.

Books everyone into a cheap chain hotel. Fair enough.

All good until it was discovered that the cheapskate had accidentally booked them into the Richmond, North Yorkshire, version.

In his defence, he apparently checked up the day before and managed to sort out the mess.

Nevertheless a "criminal" mistake.

Clearly, geography was not his strongest suit.

Meanwhile, get this.

Regarding the squad who went through the M&Js when Caolin Ryan, who went on to play first team for Moseley, Coventry, Rotherham and Chinnor, was part of the scene.

His dad, Cillian, reveals that in the aftermath of a famous victory they all "borrowed" road signs and wrote their names on them. All of which ended up in his attic.

Revolving in time some 15 years, it is 2025 and there are roadworks in Cillian's street.

So, wanting to get rid, he decides to edge the things out from the attic and merge them in, hoping nobody notices.

"But first I had to spend a night using nail varnish to remove the incriminating names," he reveals.

One hopes the authorities might yet "nail" him!

On the Back foot

The boys are returning from an international at Twickenham – Terry Fradgley, Peter Hill, Jimmy Finnegan at al.

It is decided the party should stop off at the Bear at Woodstock.

A cold evening, which gets to David Back in particular.

Puts a log on the open fire and then a load more in a bid to generate some warmth and a bonfire effect.

Maybe, as a consequence, a little over-does it.

Evacuate! Time to do a runner.

Next thing anyone knows is flames pouring out of the chimney and the siren of a fire engine coming down the road.

Pigging it

Stephen Butler is perhaps not the first name to come to mind when pondering two of Moseley's iconic moments.

The first being the 1981/82 John Player Cup Final success when he wasn't even on the pitch.

However, with the team booked to stay overnight in a hotel off the M4, the supporters reached there first and infamously ate most of the food earmarked for the players.

And guess who was in the trough – yes, Butler.

One suspects the first man to be publicly 'fingered' for his gluttony!

He was though part of the fifteen in a United game away at Leicester when he reputedly punched out Dean Richards' teeth.

"Richards was squealing like a baby," claims a source, which somewhat contradicts the England international's macho image.

Then 'all hell broke out'.

Seems Leicester were 'spitting teeth'.

Goodness knows why!

Beauties and the beast

Decades ago journeys back and forth to London were long and trying – poorer roads both to the capital and through the suburbs.

However, there were many means of amusement.

John Beale remembers: "On one such trip we got to within about three miles of the Aston Expressway when suddenly one of our younger players was 'garrotted' from behind his seat by one of the older henchmen. Other members of his group suddenly appeared, threats were made to this player's mates who were told not to interfere, and he was quickly stripped naked, tied up, his groin area blacked with boot polish and then washed down with liniment.

"By this time we were getting close to the Reddings where, we remembered, there was a disco on. When we arrived at the clubhouse the victim was carried in and set down in the middle of the dance floor in all his naked glory much to the amusement of the dancers."

Name?

Beale adds: "Anyone who is interested in what it feels like to have liniment over your testicles should ask Dave Warren!"

Which begs the question how he managed to sire three children. Clearly a miracle!

And there is a postscript.

Beale continues: "About two weeks later we had a similar trip and on the way back one of the players had heard the whisper that he was going to be a target for similar action. As we drew close to the A38(M) slip road, the coach slowed right down, the player jumped off and escaped!"

Name: Hamilton Jones.

Not everyone knows that he was picked up by a police car and dropped off on the Walsall Road. Luck had been with him. The policeman was a rugby player!

Dancing to a different tune

A chip off the old block

Gerry Acton was the comeback king, hauled in by Moseley, long after he had stepped down to his original junior club, Ludlow, whenever there was an injury crisis among the centres.

Produced newspaper headlines such as "SOS to Acton from Moseley" and "Moseley rescued again by SOS man Acton".

He explains: "Martin Green phoned me and asked if I was fit. I think it was 1971. I got the OK from Ludlow and ended up playing three games, one of which was against Coventry. My winger was Keith Fielding!"

Indeed, such was the lad's colourful rugby career that he got the Eamonn Andrews treatment.

He goes on: "Years later, when I was playing for Ludlow 4ths, the club decided unbeknown to myself to do a "This Is Your Life" on me. It was held in a big room at The Angel Hotel.

"The chairman Roger Evans had the Red Book and three Moseley players had been invited to say something – Ron Morris, Martin Hale and Peter McGowan.

"They had also gone to Jan Webster's sports shop and got a piece from him (Webster was another comeback merchant). After some hilarious other interviews came the story of me going back to Moseley and playing with one of the best players (Keith Fielding) in the country, making out he was the upcoming surprise guest!

"Instead it was a filmed interview with the winger I next played with, Ackerman Freeman, who was in a mobile fish and chip shop in Craven Arms. He slid the door open and said I never passed the ball to him so started his own business!"

Gerry was always a 'chipper' character!

 PS: Talking of chips … just for the heck of it, one of my favourite jokes … as told by John Bentley, England international at both rugby league and rugby union, and a British & Irish Lion, about his native Yorkshire.

Question: What has Cleckheaton got in common with Las Vegas?

Answer: Two of the few places in the world where you can get sex for chips!

Protherough's final game

It was the last match of the season, away at Cheltenham.

It was also hooker Dave Protherough's last game before retirement, and it was doubly special as Cheltenham was the club he had captained before moving to Moseley.

John Beale states: "For Moseley the match was a huge disappointment. Ours was a poor performance at the end of which the home side came out the winners.

"A few beers in the clubhouse soon washed away the chagrin of the loss and four of us decided to go on a small walk into Cheltenham centre for a curry. As we went out of the ground, we could see to our amusement that Proth's beaten-up old Land Rover had been covered in empty beer barrels by some of the lads.

"We got to the curry house where we enjoyed a good meal, and called for the bill. We handed over our dues to the eldest member of the group who said he would pay and catch us up. Less than five minutes later we heard a commotion from behind and shouts of 'run'! There was our bill-paying teammate with a waiter after him. We fled as fast as we could, at one point weaving around gravestones as we charged through an old churchyard. Eventually, confident that we were safe, we made our way back to the rugby club.

"Imagine our shock as we turned the corner to see our pals lined up against the wall of the ground being questioned by the occupants of a couple of police cars! It was with huge relief we found out that they weren't after curry thieves!

"It transpired that Proth, rather the worse for wear, had decided to go home. When he got to his old Land Rover he wasn't too happy to see all the casks on it, so one by one threw them off. Unfortunately, they had rolled down the ramped entrance to the ground and straight into the road where unfortunate drivers had found themselves having to dodge them."

Only Protherough could get into scrapes like that!

But, for sure, a barrel of laughs.

Boxing babes

Who was more panicked when Dave Warren's wife gave birth on Boxing Day to first child Alex than wife Jacqui or big mate John Beale.

It was touch and go for Alex, just 2lbs 2oz, 12 weeks premature, and it was touch and go for Beale whose alcohol consumption on Christmas Day had included a load of whisky, confident in the knowledge he wouldn't be facing his old club Coventry the next day.

Dave states: "I told Bealey he had to play."

Not happy.

"It was the first time I have ever drunk whisky the night before a game," declares Beale. "I'd necked a bottle of the stuff."

Derek Nutt too has convoluted memories of Boxing Day births. "I was with my heavily pregnant wife Jean spending Christmas with the in-laws in Glasgow. Nick Jeavons was after my shirt and I was determined to play on Boxing Day. Dave Warren picked me up from New Street Station about 2pm and somehow we made it to Coventry's then ground at Coundon Road."

Euphoric that in the interim he had a son, Richard.

Moseley won and the lad was supposed to turn round immediately and head back to Glasgow.

Didn't quite happen – blame Warrow for over-enthusiastic wetting of the baby's head!

Worst excuses for missing training

Graham Smith – twisted ankle falling down pothole in pavement, but did get compensation off the council!

Tee for two – no way

In the 2000s the Pons family tore through Moseley like a Brummie version of the Trotters.

Del Boy patriarch Greg, plus sons Ben, who went from Colts to the first team, and Dan, a fly half and full back with Moseley Oak.

You could never second-guess them because you never knew what Pons spectrum would turn up on the day.

Laughter, mischief, larger than life, money-making schemes, dark glasses …

So, Moseley Oak, before they marched up a few leagues, were playing Bishop's Castle, from deepest Shropshire teuchter land at home on Billesley Common.

Ten minutes or so into the game this blond lad turns up and takes his place at fly half for Castle.

Dan Pons is instantly on his case especially when he discovers that, despite originating from Bishops Castle, the kid is working in London and his name is Henry, aka Hooray Henry. Nothing posh about Pons and he is deeply suspicious of this fake toff.

Always ready to wind up the opposition, Pons is making barbed remarks throughout the match.

Which culminates in a last minute try and conversion opportunity for Henry – it wouldn't have won them the game but it would have allowed them to get something out of it.

Now, Bishops Castle either don't have or can't find their kicking tee – all a bit of a technological challenge for village yokels – so someone throws on Pons' personal one.

Pons goes ballistic … and in a flurry of swear words makes clear to Henry there is no way is he going to get use of it.

Not exactly the height of sportsmanship.

Forced to take a drop goal and misses.

As with the Latin translation of pons, a bridge too far for poor Henry.

Pons don't take prisoners!

Topper hopper

Rob Matthews was a nuclear scientist at Aston University in the late 80s and early 90s.

A second row, mostly for the United but sometimes for the first team.

And as part of his rugby 'training', whenever he was going up in a lift he would jump in the air, seeking to defy gravity, on the basis that this would improve his game, in particular his lineout ability.

"It was a theory that didn't really work," declares fellow Moseley player John Beale, himself a bit of a science junkie.

Presumably had it been today's strange world he would be part of the 'trans' community and identifying as a kangaroo!

Webster's Welsh wind-up

On Jan Webster's first away game in Wales with Moseley – only just out of nappies really – the coach made its planned stop at Strensham services southbound on the M5 for refreshments and a leg stretch.

When everyone had returned, skipper Nigel Horton asked his usual stupid question "does everyone have their passport in readiness to cross the border into Wales"?

Ho, ho, ho.

Jan, raw, young, maybe a touch overawed, replied in the negative, worry spreading across his face.

Much fake consternation from his more knowledgeable and experienced brethren.

Informed how in that case he would have to be smuggled in.

Completely bought the wind-up, hook, line and sinker.

Former first teamer Ian Bowland comments: "He was escorted by Nigel into the boot of the bus where he was told to be super quiet to avoid discovery."

And the poor innocent, packed in with the kit, was non-the wiser after the match either.

Ian goes on: "An excellent victory in Wales had no impact upon the protocols and Jan was returned to the boot for the border crossing back into England. Delighted to be released upon arrival at Strensham services northbound!"

Myth?

We can't ask Jan who passed on several years back, much lamented.

It wasn't actually Ian's era so he didn't witness it, but, after investigation, is confident it did take place.

Jan Webster

Jan's long time fly half partner Martin Cooper, who at that time "had just managed to get into Wolverhampton's third team", thinks it all "unlikely".

Nigel claims no recollection. "Sounds a good story. It could have happened – so many things went on in those days."

Nice to think it did.

Either way his Moseley education progressed quickly and he didn't stay naïve for long!

Do as I say; not what I do

I am beginning to think there should have been an entire 'bloopers' book on John White alone.

Anyway, here's another one for your amusement.

Pre-season in the 1980s always culminated with a Bank Holiday training weekend in Exeter hosted by the very talented ex Moseley flyer Keith Hatter. Where Moseley training on Saturday and Sunday was followed by a series of games against Exeter on the Monday (Moseley winning every one by a cricket score – how times change).

In August 1983, Whitey explains to the players the need for all of the group and coaches to focus, maximise effort, and concentrate at all times to obtain the most benefit from an opportunity to be in a healthy environment and lifestyle.

My spy states: "Before we arrived in Devon he concluded his key messages with the clear statement 'this is emphatically not a piss up'.

"The following morning at approximately 3.30am in Keith Hatter's hotel snug bar, Whitey fell backwards off his stool!"

Unsurprisingly, that day at training no one mentioned the rumble and a tumble.

Gamekeeper turned poacher

We can't leave Phil Hall out of this book – the man with the howler monkey voice.

The sound travels way out of the stand and half way to the Malvern Hills.

He writes: "In the distant past I was (the long-suffering) match secretary for the Nomads, the Wanderers and the Vandals.

"As was customary, I had my three teams confirmed by Monday of each week. As was also customary, by the Friday night/Saturday morning I was scratching around to fill the gaps given the 1st and 2nd team players dropping out due to injury – perhaps even the odd broken finger nail.

"On too many occasions I had to cancel the Vandals fixture because I did not have enough able bodied left to make a half team, never mind a full team.

"Sadly, some players returning from injury simply refused to appear for any team lower than United, which didn't help my cause. By contrast, some seasoned first teamers including Warro, Derek Nutt, John Beale, Peter Shillingford and even Nick Jeavons would turn out for the Wanderers – even the Vandals on occasion – and that was always greatly appreciated."

He goes on: "By contrast there were those in the junior ranks who would play for a higher team at the drop of a hat – even if they did have a broken finger nail. One was me!

"Barely credence then that I, a former schoolboy rugby league winger, had a late in the week, late night telephone call from no other than John White, the first team coach, asking me if I would play for the Nomads at Harlequins. I told him he must be desperate if he wanted me on the wing for the Nomads and away to Harlequins to boot.

"Typical I had got it all wrong. Phew! Then he said he didn't want me to play on the wing, he wanted me to play hooker. God forbid times were indeed desperate if I had been asked to play hooker at Harlequins."

Wake up and smell the liniment!

"Well at the first scrum – there was no touch, set, engage in those days – the front rows crashed together and my swede was on the wrong side of the opposing hooker. He politely asked me to get my flipping head out of the flipping way, or he would wrench the flipping thing off my shoulders – or words to that effect.

"We reset. It was our put-in so in came the ball, down the middle in those days, not behind the second row …

"Well, before I had even thought about attempting to hook it, there was a flash of a foot and it disappeared into the Harlequins midst."

However, a sting in the tale.

"Just as the ref blew 'foot up', a gruff Scottish command came from the Harlequins second row. 'You don't do that at this level laddie.' It was no other than Bill Cuthbertson (21 caps for Scotland). Although I won all my scrums from thereon, we still lost."

Great memories are as much the result of defeats as victories!

Strong-armed

John White's learning curve …

Studying at higher education establishment St Paul's College in Cheltenham, but sometimes hauled in to turn out for Moseley.

Maiden first team game against Northampton at the Reddings. Playing No.8. Around 1963.

Northampton put the ball into a scrum on the Moseley 25 yard line and duly win it.

Whitey, in his youthful enthusiasm, all geared up to 'corner flag'.

"Suddenly these arms come over and grab my shirt and neck. Then other arms follow and take hold of the other side. Followed by the remark 'where the %*!+ do you think you're going'."

Welcome to elite rugby.

PS: At least somehow Moseley stopped a try being scored!

Pole-axed

The Dark Ages when the motoring laws were somewhat more relaxed and rugby players were allowed to banter with coach drivers …

Occasionally they would have a pint with you before setting off for home – generally a fair bit of leeway.

The team had been to the West Country to play Bristol, good humour on the return journey and somehow England three-quarter Colin McFadyean persuades the driver to let him take charge of the last 200 yards from Alcester Road into Reddings Road and back to the clubhouse.

Except McFadyean has never driven a 42ft coach before and botches the left turn manoeuvre, bringing the vehicle into contact with a telegraph pole.

But he's in luck.

John White recalls: "He clipped the pole perfectly and took it clean out of the ground while hardly damaging the coach at all."

Conspiracy of silence from all concerned (especially the driver) and days before baffled workmen got round to putting it back up.

The sound of music

This is the story of how Phil Hall, the Moseley Pavarotti, has inspired many a home side to greatness.

All down to the Moseley 'call' which he could hold for so long it seemed to go on forever and always hailed by a cheer from surrounding supporters when finally ended.

The secret? An 'operatic' bent because during the early 70s he 'trod the boards' with Queensbridge Operatic Society.

Strictly amateur, but had he been born several decades later it is nice to speculate that he just might have rivalled Wayne Evans at Go.Compare.

He states (non-music buffs fingers in ears): "The first opera I did was Land of Smiles, a romantic operetta, by Franz Lehar, with its signature tune, You are my Heart's Delight made famous by the tenor, Richard Tauber. I have also performed in two other operetta, La Belle Helene and Merry England. I have never had any desire to sing anything Gilbert and Sullivan!"

Now we get to the interesting stuff ...

"It was during those days that I learned to project my voice and somewhere along the road that ability blossomed in the Reddings stand at Moseley Rugby Club.

"I rather suspect that of the many games I attended I picked up on visiting supporters urging their team on 'musically' and, being somewhat competitive, thought I could match them. Before too long I not only matched them in volume but surpassed them in duration. Indeed it was quite pleasing to 'compete' against visiting supporters and hear them fade away exhausted whilst I sailed merrily on.

"My pitch is based on the starting note of Nessun Dorma – middle C – as sung by Luciano Pavarotti. He could also sing the final note – top C – and it was here where I would try to match and stay with him for that last climax, something I rarely achieved."

Such was Phil's fame – or maybe infamy – some years ago a competition was held at Moseley with bets taken on how long he could hold the note. "I think my best ever was around 1 minute 10 seconds. Now, a lot older, 30 seconds or so is about my limit."

Nevertheless, there's a punchline.

"The BBC have even recorded me because if you watch and listen to the video of the 18th April 2009 EDF Cup Final at Twickenham you will hear me.

"I have yet to receive royalties!"

Hat-trick hero

The lads have been in the North-west and on departure descend on this chip shop.

Les Smith, second row, big man, bit of a charmer, is leading the mischief while waiting in line to be served. All fun and games.

Anyway, there's this local wearing a scruffy cap, which Les decides to purloin.

So, the cap is doing the rounds with the players, its owner pleading for its return, everyone still in good spirits.

Meantime Les has reached the head of the queue.

John White takes up the story. "He says to the assistant 'I'd like battered hat and chips please'."

What? Blank looks all round.

"So, Les dips this hat in the batter and chucks it into the chip fat."

It would be nice to report this sparked a gigantic brawl but apparently the stunt was taken in good humour and Les pacified the bloke whose cap it was by giving him his scarf!

Bottoms Up

Some real old Moseley lags – John Richards, Andy Johnson, Tim Elt and Ian Bowland, all on another one of those Canada tours.

They arrive at the premier local tennis club for a hit, sauna, gym etc.

Bowland reports: "John had purchased new trainers for the occasion and took huge delight in rolling the surrounding tissue paper up into a big ball and walking over to another member of our group who was getting changed, pulled his pants out from behind and stuffed in the said tissue paper with a loud yell of 'whahey' followed by a quick cheek grope."

Like in the Falklands, a shocked Bowland counted them in and counted them out – John, check; Andy, check; Tim, check; and himself, check.

Who might be the 'fifth columnist'?

The victim, it transpired, was supposed to be Elt … except it wasn't.

Bowland goes on: "All three of us watched it unfold, unable to do anything, knowing the mistake John was making, a Sam Peckinpah movie scene in slow motion. It left this future president of MRFC, completely mortified, trying to explain the 'stuffing' to an apoplectic Canadian and total stranger."

Of course, no sympathy from the tourists for their colleague's predicament.

"None of us could actually play any tennis or work out because our stomachs were too painful from the laughing spasms. Tears were pouring from our eyes."

PS: JR is at some rugby lunch and for a laugh is bent on setting up this guy who loathes public speaking.

So, there is our man on his feet, giving his spiel, which incidentally he is very good at, when he announces, words to the effect, "I now hand over to Fred Bloggs (he professes to have forgotten the name, if you believe that) who will further enlighten you."

Petrified, the bloke diffidently stands up and states: "I only know two long words – corrugated and marmalade."

And sits down!

Thoroughly marmalated.

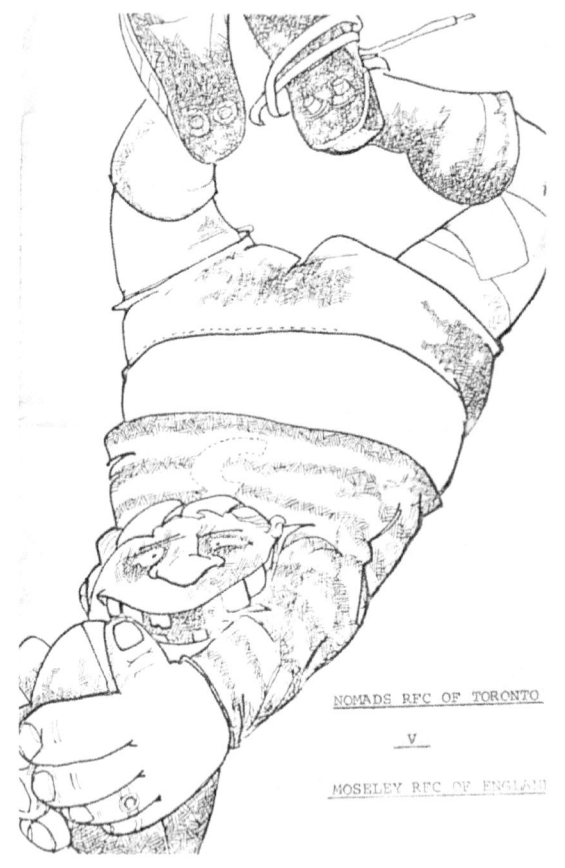

Practice makes perfect

Screwing the system

Once when security was far from tight there was ways and means of getting into internationals for peanuts.

The great England star and Moseley captain Peter Robbins had somehow gained the honour of being a Freeman of Paris.

So he goes up to this gendarme on the entrance gate, explains who he is, and the guy is so impressed he allows 22 of PGD's mates, including Gerry Acton and Warwickshire and England cricketer MJK Smith, to gain entrance for nothing.

Of course, none of them had seats and simply sat on the concrete and watched the match.

Top. G.I. JOKER... alias Robbins with David Bucknall & Major Robert Cotterell

Bottom. STRANDED IN PARIS...

Robbins trying to make the best of a long at De Gaulle Airport with Messieurs, Cl Parsons, Martin Oliver, Gerry Acton, th author, Derek Fowler & MJK Smith

Peter Robbins holding court at Charles de Gaulle Airport along with fellow luminaries including Gerry Acton, David Bucknall and MJK Smith

Mind you, Acton, who had printing connections, had his own scam – for getting into Twickenham.

Well, not actually fake tickets to the ground, but the troops did print their own car park entry forms, which at least gave them a head start.

Gerry reveals: "In about 1972/73 Peter had a North Car Park permit which was a piece of white gummed paper 6 inches by 6 with a large blue chevron on it with black type. He said it would be a wheeze if I could print three tickets and we could all picnic together. I changed the number from his original ticket and we duly picnicked with no problem.

"Anyway, we got away with it for years even though one time I didn't have an original ticket and put a diamond blue shape when it was a chevron. They didn't notice."

The odd query from Plod, but nothing to get overly concerned about.

I seem to recall that Greville Edwards had his own slippery tactics for entry to the East car park.

An amazing food and booze pitch. His pork pies were to die for.

Worth every moment of lies and obfuscation!

Giving JPR the run-around

James Jowett, pivotal in getting Moseley to Billesley Common and building up the club from there, is on the Lions Tour to South Africa June/July 2009 with sons Spencer and Ben.

Touring about in a motorhome they have dubbed "Hotel du Van".

Venue – Kings Park, Durban – Second Test. The pre-match celebrations – drinks, banter and braai's (monster Afrikaans BBQ's) – are in full swing when he bumps into JPR Williams, the old Welsh great.

James takes up the story …

"About an hour or so to kick off JPR comes into sight walking through the car park and in my direction. I had met him briefly a couple of times previously back in the day when we regularly played London Welsh. As he drew closer, he had this look on his face which suggested 'I think I know this guy but who the f**k is he' and to save him any embarrassment I introduced myself and shook his hand.

"Beers and chat followed and then he announces that he must leave as he is working as pundit for one of the TV channels/newspapers and due at a pre-match press briefing in the south stand."

Which is the south stand, he inquires.

"Well, having achieved A level geography many years previously, I competently point him in the right direction and say good bye."

All sorted, except …

James goes on: "Shortly after we go to enter the ground and having negotiated the turnstiles a helpful ground steward asks in broad Bokkie accent 'which stand are you in' and knowingly I look at the ticket and point to the south stand. 'No!' he retorts – 'you're in the southern hemisphere now mate, it's at the other end'! Whereupon we turn around in hasty retreat, also feeling guilty at misdirecting JPR, hoping he eventually found his way to the correct venue!"

James Jowett and JPR

But, did he?

James goes on: "Cue MRC autumn supper in the old clubhouse later that year. Guest speaker is John Taylor, great open side flanker for London Welsh/Wales/Lions but also a great friend of JPR and best man at his wedding. After supper, I engage with JT at the bar and during the conversation ask if he sees much of JPR these days. Response 'yes, we keep in touch but the last time we met was in

Durban, South Africa, for the Lions Test at the pre-match press briefing when as usual he turned up late'. JT continues – 'JPR was regularly late but always had some excuse and this time he told us that some idiot in the car park had sent him to the wrong stand'!"

At which James plays the innocent.

"Would you like another drink, John, ask I?"

Enter stage left

Rugby folk and art luvvies tend to look down on each other ... just occasionally they mix.

So, back in the day, you would from time to time find Richard Burton and Elizabeth Taylor at London Welsh, the former, as a Welshman, being a big fan of the game.

Down at Rosslyn Park you might bump into Oliver Reed, a member there who sometimes turned out for the club.

Burton and Reed, both with a deserved reputation for hell-raising, sadly no longer with us.

Perhaps the closest Birmingham Moseley has come in recent times to a celebrity is Richard Stott, detective inspector in the police, appearing on popular ITV competition The Chase.

A bit of a Moseley hero – record number of appearances for the club over 12 seasons, lifted the EDF National Trophy at Twickenham, plus a significant player for both the British Police and England Counties.

Unfortunately blown away by the Chaser, £5,000 down the drain.

One hopes his police chases are rather more successful!

Sex and Cities

Finally, we couldn't really end without a bit more sex.

And, of course, that means tourists out of control.

A voyeur states: "The locals encountered on our first Junior tour to Canada proved to be some of the most accommodating ever and friendships, and cooperation over business, continued for years after.

"The supreme example was when one of our front row forwards found out that the girlfriend of one of them (Hal Rowan) was an old flame. Well the flame apparently had not died. The next day Hal complains to the touring team that he was not happy about this individual sleeping with his woman but he supposed it was all part of being a good host. However, he did object to him using his personal toothbrush that he had left at her house!"

As an addendum, my mole continues: "He would have made an official complaint about this to our tour manager – but that was the culprit!"

Plenty more porn.

"The same Canadian hosts in Toronto also laid on a private strip show in one of their houses and another of our front three took a full and active part in satisfying the invitation of one of the girls in front of the watching audience. There was some debate as to whether this was when our man lost his virginity, but he claimed not."

Meanwhile …

"On another tour, this time to New England, we stayed with different sets of hosts in the three places we were playing – Boston, Dover and Worcester. Alan Hill (part of the Hill dynasty with Peter, Steve and Jonathan) has always been a lothario who looked for a 'a girl in every port' and when it came to the farewell bash three different ladies from each of the tour venues turned up to see him off. Alan being Alan took it all in his stride."

Well, that's one way of putting it!

SNITCHES

John Duckers, John Beale, Dave Warren, John Nolan, Roy Kerr, Jonathan Duckers, Dave Allen, Lee Evans, Peter Veitch, Barrie Williams, Mike Gair, James Jowett, Bob Brown, Tony Kenny, Ron Morris, Harley Williams, Barbara Challinor, Derek Nutt, Bill Sweeney, Ollie Thomas, Robin Johnson, Gary Baldwin, Martin Crutchley, Dick Goodman, Dave Thomas, John Lamb, Joanne Malin, Allen Jenkins, Alan Cull, Bob Bannister, Tony Bertram, Jack Richards, Cillian Ryan, Gerry Acton, Gavin Petrie, Ian Bowland, John White, Andy Arnott, Joe Henderson, Richard Davies, Nigel Horton, Trevor Bow.

Printed in Great Britain
by Amazon